An Open Secret

A Student's Handbook for Learning Aikido Techniques of Self-Defense and the Aiki Way

Tony M. Blomert

A&E Blomert Enterprises, LLC
1304 Wineglass Lane
Livingston, MT 59047

A&E Blomert Enterprises, LLC
1304 Wineglass Lane
Livingston, MT 59047
www.aikidotoday.com

An Open Secret/Tony M. Blomert
1st edition
ISBN: 978-1503093522

DISCLAIMER:
Please note that the publisher and author of this instructional book are not responsible in any manner whatsoever for any injury that may result from practicing the techniques and/or following the instructions given within.

Martial arts training can be dangerous to you and to others if not practiced safely. If you're in doubt as to how to proceed or whether your practice is safe, please consult with a trained martial arts instructor before beginning. Since the physical activities described herein may be too strenuous in nature for some readers, it's also essential that a physician be consulted prior to training.

Best efforts have been used in preparing this material which is presented solely within this book for educational purposes. The author and publisher make no representations or warranties of

Book Layout and Editing by Mary Jo Stresky, The Write MoJo Literary and Research Services (www.thewritemojo.com)

Photographs by Eva J. Blomert, Big Sky Graphic

Photo Models: Aaron Anderes, Kelly Goebel, Wells Nishimoto, Rajesh Patel, Joshua Puskarich, Emmanuel Santos, Satoru Sato

Dedication

"Even when still, your mind is not still; even when hurried, your mind is not hurried. Even if superficially weak-hearted, be inwardly strong-hearted, and do not let others see into your mind."
~Miyamoto Musashi, Japan (1643)

I wish to dedicate my book to Dr. Lynn D. Lomen (1927-2011) who was my teacher, counselor and friend.

**(Dr. Lomen on your right –
young Tony on your left – Circa 1975)**

Acknowledgements

It took the efforts of many talented people and extensive informational sources to produce this book, so I want to thank all of you for your amazing contributions.

Also to the training partners I've had the pleasure to work with over the years, *domo arigato gozaimashita*!

There are a few individuals who must be singled out for a special acknowledgement:
First is my spouse and partner, Eva Blomert, for her constant encouragement and patience, as well as wonderful photography.

Mary Jo Stresky (thewritemojo.com) for helping to craft the words you are about to read into understandable clarity.

My heartfelt thanks go to Kelly Goebel and Manny Santos for their demonstration assistance throughout this book. And to the Shidokan dojo in Las Vegas, Nevada, as well as the Big Sky Aikido in Bozeman, Montana, for use of their well-appointed facilities.

I can't express enough gratitude to my teachers for their guidance throughout my Aikido journey: William Gleason, Hiroshi Ikeda, George Ledyard, Dr. Lynn Lomen, John Messores, Gregory Olson and James Sterling.

Thank you, Shihan Mitsugi Saotome, for your vision, insight and providing the organizational structure that nurtured my education.

Finally, I wish to express my most sincere gratitude and respect to **Morihei Ueshiba**, the Founder of Aikido, for giving us all a path to follow.

Contents

Preface

While seated on the floor in total stillness, I am filled with a sense of tranquility. An *ikebana* arrangement sits graceful against the rich wood paneled backdrop of the *shomen*. A portrait of the founder (O'Sensei), appearing simultaneously serene and stern, seems to be focused solely on me.

Glancing just off center at the display of weaponry, I realize the simplicity of the room is very deceiving. These surroundings have hundreds of years of tradition, and obvious and hidden meanings are everywhere.

This appointed time and place to demonstrate what I'd learned after years of study for my *dan* exam has been years in coming. I contemplate the task at hand, and then clear my mind of all thought. There is only breath. My breath -- life's breath.

Breathe ... blink ... breathe.

The sweltering air has grown heavy with humidity, and I realize that I'm in a different time and place.

It's mid-summer in feudal Japan in the year 1629. I'm standing on one side of a rope and plank bridge spanning a treacherous river below. As I begin crossing over the single person-wide path, I see a man standing on the opposite end who's also beginning to cross over.

We have instant recognition. We are *aite* (opponents), and are both in *samurai* dress with *daisho* (*katana* and *wakizashi*). Sunlight glints off the highly polished steel blades of my swords. Each receiving one thousand blessings from the *kami*, they had been forged and honed while the smithy made the offerings.

The drama unfolds as we both continue our paths across the bridge. Neither of us can or will yield by turning back, and therefore only one will cross alive. There is only one way for matched warriors to achieve victory: *The first to take the space!*

Breathe ... blink.

The air feels cool on my skin as my mind returns to the present. The noisy chatter of over fifty students engulfs the room, and they go silent as the panel of *Shihan* enter. The quiet is broken by the calling of my name for the examination. The next hour is a replay of that fateful moment in 1629, but this time without any bloodshed.

Long afterwards I sit alone on the floor again in deep contemplation. My thoughts first focus on the tasks I just completed, and then journey on to what is beginning anew.

Breathe...

4 · TONY M. BLOMERT

Introduction

I was introduced to Aikido when I was a wide-eyed 17-year-old high school senior attending a pre-college summer session at Los Angeles Valley College. Back then Aikido was still considered a "new" martial art, but is now a mainstream *budo* practiced around the world.

That first class transformed my life as the **Aiki** principles became the foundation upon which my adult existence would be built. Taking those lessons to heart allowed me to stand calmly observant in the eye of life's storms. I learned to become aware of what lie ahead, and then react with an appropriate response.

Most people today – myself included -- no longer have to deal with constant life or death circumstances their ancestors faced. But being able to handle the circumstances that are part of the modern world still presents challenges such as success and failure, happiness and loneliness, gains and loss, and accepting the ultimate finality of death.

There have been a few changes to the Aikido dojo these past decades, the most significant of which has been its "face" as the majority of practitioners and instructors today are non-Japanese.

Several thousand dojos now are run by instructors originating from the country and towns the dojo is located in (i.e., from Honolulu to Istanbul, Mexico City to Tel Aviv, Cape Town to Rio de Janeiro). While today's Aikido dojo has a localized definition, they still hold tightly to Japanese tradition.

The terminology currently used was developed in part due to a clearer translation of Japanese meanings into English and other languages. Certain words are a result of common usage, as language modifies itself to fit the times.

For example, students who seriously train and follow the Aiki way are now referred to as *Aikidoka*. Scholars and linguists may argue the various implications of this moniker, because it has become widely used as an acceptable description for those who live the Aiki lifestyle, and is no longer reserved for those few professionals making a living teaching.

Why the Title "An Open Secret"?

Aikido and all the martial arts are shrouded by the mystique of Asian lore and nuances. This fact lends itself to situations and knowledge that are often left unspoken. Information is provided by a Sensei to those individuals who have practiced an art for many years and are deemed worthy, and even then the knowledge is imparted in less than a straightforward method. For people raised in a Western culture, this is contrary to how they usually experience most of their educational learning.

Experienced students and masters of the art know the information, but keep it as "**an open secret**" among themselves. It just isn't discussed, unless a situation calls for discourse and disclosure.

Most of the really important subject matter in the martial arts is handled in this fashion. Even when a technique is being demonstrated, seldom are the true secrets revealed of what makes the technique work (I personally don't agree with this teaching style because it doesn't work in general for most non-Asians).

There are details that definitely need to be withheld until a student is ready to fully grasp the information. I equate it along the lines of having a basic education before being able to handle college level courses. One first needs to crawl before learning how to stand and walk, and then they learn how to run.

Then there are some who are capable and desirous of learning how to run better, faster, longer and become an Olympic level competitor. How well one develops the necessary skills determines whether a student will have the ability to handle more complex studies.

Aikido must be *felt* and *experienced*. The Aiki spirit translates into the strength within oneself to not do fatal harm, a peaceful solution to conflict, to follow the energy of the situation rather than travel a predetermined course of action, not forcing a particular approach, not using brute force and other similar descriptions.

While this may appear to be non-aggressive, true Aiki is very energetic and comes from core strength. This may sound contradictory on the surface, which is why it is an art that requires hands-on experience.

My Purpose for Writing This Book

An Open Secret represents a substantial milestone on the journey I began many years ago. My life has had its share of highs, lows and plateaus, so I want to offer a roadmap for readers to follow as they travel their own path.

Although I share insights into common practices and customs found at a typical Aikido dojo, I won't be including information about many of the techniques as the able instructors at a dojo teach those best.

However, I will be covering a variety of equally important topics that are usually learned through word of mouth, personal experience, or a scolding by Sensei after having made a breach of etiquette or causing some offense. (These types of educational sources from others often propagate myths. Although they may be well-meaning, they often provide erroneous, incomplete information that can misinform a student of the art.)

My purpose is to help students develop a better understanding of common etiquette, their responsibilities, dojo design, apparel, the relationship between student and teacher and between students, training tools and weapons, rank examination, the Aiki spirit, and fundamental training concepts. And finally, some proven tips that have helped me and others develop our Aikido skills.

I will cite historical and philosophical reasons for chosen practices and topics that are frequently asked by beginning and experienced students. I've also laced this information with some of my own anecdotes and experiences.

Rather than being a definitive tome, **An Open Secret** strives to be a starting point for students to develop their own understanding of Aikido dojo customs since practices are always evolving. Where appropriate, it will address current trends and old school, more traditional approaches.

Naturally, dojo and instructor interpretations of Aikido will vary. The state of today's practice has progressed sufficiently to include all forms of variations from the traditional approach. No unanimous agreement exists on the correct way to do much of anything in life, so in this regard the Aikido community is no exception.

How to Use This Book

An Open Secret solves the mystery of Aikido by including factual truths, historical reasonings, and detailed explanations of etiquette required of all students.

It takes an in-depth look at the common and unique practices all Aikidoka (practitioners of Aikido) need to know; the background of Aikido's rich history as *budo* (martial art); a current assessment of the art's international status; and an overview of various sub-styles in the 21st century.

Most importantly, the *An Open Secret* provides a proven learning methodology that can be used by women, men, children and seniors alike, and can become a permanent lifestyle for improved physical and spiritual health.

Other topics include step-by-step pointers on selection and care of the uniform (the Aikido *gi* and *hakama*), equipment (Aikido weapons – *jo* and *bokken*), and the training facility (Aikido dojo).

Grading and promotion examination details are covered for both beginning and advanced students. Students' progressive responsibilities as they advance in rank and experience are also described.

You should use *An Open Secret* as a practical guide to most training situations and general knowledge, as it's designed to give you a better understanding of the reasons behind certain practices.

Being armed with many different kinds of techniques and traditions of Aikido will help you enjoy a more joyful training experience!

Think of this learning manual as a seasoned co-worker who teaches you the ropes through their wisdom and experience, and respects you enough to pull you aside before you do something your boss could punish you for. It will be your guide, your comrade-in-arms, your tutor and your mentor.

While you may take different routes, your destination is the same. Whether you're just beginning your Aiki journey, or you've already been traveling the path, keep in mind that there are many ways to get to the top of the mountain. Assuredly there will be a few roadblocks and wrong turns along the way, but a truthful, dedicated effort will result in many enjoyable rewards.

For more information on Tony Blomert and his Aikido program and products: www.aikidotoday.com

CHAPTER ONE

What is Aikido?

Morihei Ueshiba (1883-1969) founded the martial art known today as Aikido. To those who practice the art, he is reverently referred to as O'Sensei (Great Teacher).

Based on a rich heritage of various Japanese combat techniques, Aikido seeks to unify with life energy to defend oneself and to also protect the attacker. The word *Aikido* is formed with three *kanji* (symbolic Japanese words):

1. 合 – *ai* – joining, unifying, combining, fit
2. 気 – *ki* – spirit, energy, mood, morale
3. 道 – *dō* – way, path

O'Sensei envisioned his art as a synthesis of his personal *budo* (the lifestyle one lives and the path they walk by practicing a *bujutsu* -- a Japanese martial art developed by *samurai* warriors over 800 years ago), philosophy and religious beliefs.

The Aikido of today has developed into a number of styles with broad ranges of interpretation and emphasis by the Founder's senior students who spread the art across the globe in the late 20th century.

Aikido's primary technical influence came from *Daito-ryu Jujutsu*. However, Aikido derives much of its technical structure from the art of swordsmanship (*kenjutsu*), even though most techniques are empty-handed without a sword.

Hand-painted Woodblock Print of Miyamoto Musashi (1584-1645)

Miyamoto Musashi (aka: Shinmen Takezō, Miyamoto Bennosuke, or by his Buddhist name, Niten Dōraku) was a Japanese swordsman and rōnin. Musashi, as he was often simply known, became renowned through stories of his excellent swordsmanship in numerous duels, even from a very young age.

He was the founder of the Hyōhō Niten Ichi-ryū or Niten-ryū style of swordsmanship and the author of *The Book of Five Rings*, a book on strategy, tactics, and philosophy that is still studied today (please go to *Want to Get Aikido-Related Items?* at the end of the book to find out how to download a free copy of *Five Rings*.)

Self-Defense, Physical Fitness and Spiritual Enrichment

The relevance of Aikido in today's modern world is in the physical health and spiritual well-being of those who practice the art. The physicality consists of the coordinated use of the whole body through controlled relaxation, flexibility and endurance. Training is suitable for people of all ages, which is a main reason for Aikido's popularity.

Aikido techniques (*waza*) consist of throws and pins as self-defense from attacks that include both strikes and grabs. Students learn how to safely fall or roll to avoid injury from the techniques.

Physical training consists primarily of two partners practicing prearranged forms (*kata*). The person receiving the technique – and the one who will initiate the attack -- is referred to as *uke* or *aite*. The other partner, who applies the technique, is referred to either as *tori* or *shite*, or *nage* when the technique involves throwing.

The reason for various names is due to Aikido sub-styles that may use one or more terms. Since Aikidoka combines the principles of blending and adaptation, both roles of attacker and defender are essential to training.

Nage blends with and controls the attacking energy, while *uke* becomes calm and flexible in the disadvantageous positions in which the *nage* places them.

This receiving of the technique is called *ukemi*. *Uke* has an active rather than passive role. Their eventual fall is part of Aikido, and is a way for them to safely receive what would otherwise be a devastating strike or throw.

Uke continuously seeks to regain balance and protect any vulnerability, while *nage* uses position and timing to keep *uke* off-balance and vulnerable. Advanced training will sometimes include *uke* applying reversal techniques (*kaeshi waza*) to regain balance, and pin or throw *nage*.

Aikido also utilizes multiple attacker (*randori*) techniques and freestyle training (*jiyu waza*), usually after students have developed a proficiency of basic techniques (*kihon waza*)

Over time, the frequent and consistent Aikido training leads to the development of one's spirit. *Ki's* (aka: *qi* or *chi*) life energy principles are a part of most sub-styles of Aikido. Emphasis varies on the style, but generally techniques are powered with an extension of *ki* by the practitioner.

While de-emphasized in some sub-styles, training exercises designed to develop spiritual and self-realization continue as part of Aikido today.

The following pages explore the Aikido dojo and training in greater detail.

CHAPTER TWO

Aikido Class Basics

Morihei Ueshiba, the Founder of Aikido (aka: O'Sensei), was by all accounts an extraordinary human being and martial artist, and frequently used the expression "faster than light" when describing his theory behind Aikido.

O'Sensei often referred to his experience of being trapped in a small valley being attacked by Chinese militia (1924 – *The Great Mongolian Adventure: Omoto-kyo expedition to find Shambhala*). He was able to dodge the oncoming barrage of bullets by sensing beams of light indicating their paths of flight. He realized that to perceive an attack and avoid it was the essence of *aiki*, or the art of harmonization.

(The kanji symbol for *hikari* (light) is featured on this book's cover and referenced throughout the text. Its selection is used here in the Western sense of "shedding light" on a subject.)

Variations in Japanese and Western Manners

Let's shed some light on Aikido as a modern *budo* (in these terms *budo* translates into a "martial way of life" that encompasses both the physical art of war and the spiritual essence needed to develop one's mind, soul and body). This art utilizes a unique approach that precludes some of the traditional Japanese martial concepts, as well as the social etiquette that differs between men and women.

A certain latitude is taken concerning most etiquette and procedures in Aikido, which becomes readily apparent when comparing practices from one dojo to another. Sensei interpretations tend to vary, and local customs may overrule the general etiquette described here.

My body today suffers from what I refer to as youthful enthusiasm pushing my physical limits that resulted in stiff arm joints and worn out knees. During my early years of training in Aikido I'd massage these areas out of habit, and never noticed I was placing my hands on the front of my thighs while making a standing bow.

Among the most frequent variations are the social differences afforded Japanese men and women. This fact was painfully (and embarrassedly) explained to me when I was taken aside by Sensei when he noticed I repeatedly made that faux pas. He informed me that unless I was planning a transgender procedure, that this was a major error in etiquette.

It's socially proper for Japanese women to make a formal standing bow with their hands placed on the front of their thighs rather than on their sides.

Men however, must always have their hands on their sides. As a side note, women are also required to wear a *hakama* for modesty, while men may not be allowed the privilege until they attain a black belt rank.

People raised in a Western culture face many challenges while learning an Asian martial art. Among these hurdles are accommodating significantly different cultural manners related to proper greeting manners, how to address others, not wearing shoes indoors, and sitting on the floor, just to mention a few.

Many may argue that polite manners are lost on the current generation of youth in both Asian and Western societies. However, in the dojo culture politeness continues to be central in everything students do.

For example, upon arrival at the dojo or training location, people will notice an area near the doorway for items such as shoes, coats, etc., which makes this distinct from the training area. A dojo observes the Japanese custom of not wearing shoes indoors, so everyone must take them off and store them in this area with the heels facing the wall.

While this book is about Aikido training practices, a general understanding of traditional Japanese social graces is very good to have. For example, bowing is always a sign of respect.

As they move from the entrance into the training area, it's customary for everyone to make a formal standing bow towards the *shomen* or front of the dojo, and the same is done when exiting the dojo.

The Shomen

If there's no formal front -- such as when training outdoors or in the community room -- the person bows towards the center of the training area.

Bowing

People quickly learn that a bow is one of the most significant physical aspects of dojo etiquette. It can be very confusing for Westerners to know when and how, and to whom or what they should bow. The following guide should help in most situations encountered in a dojo.

All bows never include touching of any kind, and should be performed with the utmost courtesy and respect. You'll need to follow the etiquette rules at whatever particular dojo you attend.

Bowing practices are an acknowledgement towards the place you train at, the art itself, the Founder, the head instructor and class instructor, and the individuals with whom you'll practice.

My initial training was at a very strict traditional dojo. Students quickly learned to err on the side of more than less when it came to etiquette, since Sensei's verbal lashings can be harsh. Now I follow the adage that "one can never be too polite," and bow at almost everything and everyone.

When I moved to a new city, I was surprised at the informality of my new dojo. Though most basic bowing etiquette was followed, I was taken aside by Sensei and told that he preferred I not be so formal all the time since he wanted us to save time for training.

When in Rome do as the Romans do. So I compromised a bit of my strict etiquette by not bowing between changing roles with my training partners.

Although a bow in the dojo is an acknowledgement, it doesn't convey any religious connotation or mean to be subservient as some non-Asians would believe.

The meaning of the bow can range from a Western greeting with a hand wave gesture, shaking hands, or a formal salute. The bow can convey anything from these types of acknowledgements to a deep expression of respect and homage.

Other martial arts styles such as Aiki Jitsu, Brazilian Jiu Jitsu, Hapkido, Kung Fu, Karate, Wing Chun and their variations have very different practices and traditions. Bowing in Japan follows a strict social etiquette that could fill volumes.

But for my purpose here I'll only cover those situations common to the Aikido dojo etiquette.

When to Bow

Standing Formal Bow

Stand with your feet close together and hand palms flat to your sides. This position of informal attention maintains a straight back and shoulders, and head up facing forward. Bend forward to approximately a 45-degree angle at the waist without letting your arms move or leaving your side. Hold this for a few seconds, then straighten.

You should maintain direct eye contact when bowing towards a training partner. When bowing towards Sensei or the *shomen*, your eyes should be focused downward.

Seated Bow

The seated bow is known as *zarei*. Begin by sitting in *seiza* (see Sitting and Standing below). Initiate the bow by placing both hands on the floor in front of you with your palms down and fingers extended at an approximate 45-degree angle (see close-up photo); then bend at the waist head moving towards your hands. Keep your eyes and face straight ahead while bending towards the floor.

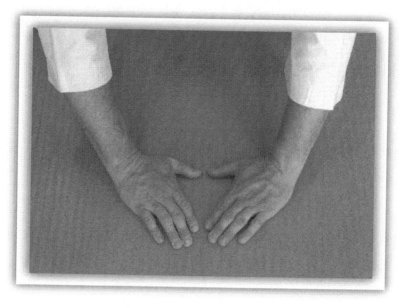

When bowing towards someone, a variation is the Japanese custom of the junior person (*kohai*) bowing slightly more than the senior person (*senpai*) as demonstrated in the photo below. It's also considered polite etiquette to avert one's eyes downward.

While this may be socially acceptable, it is more in keeping with the *budo* (warrior) spirit to maintain eye contact when bowing towards a training partner (as shown in the standing formal bow photo above). Always be alert and vigilant of a possible attack.

Sitting and Standing

Seiza literally means a "true or correct sitting." Native Japanese sit in *seiza* with their legs folded underneath their body and resting on their ankles. A humorous anecdote is that Japanese children learn *seiza* and are bowing from the time they're in their mother's womb. When the mother sits and bows during her pregnancy, so does the child.

Sitting in this manner is normal for the Japanese; however, Westerners are unaccustomed to kneeling in this position. But Aikido training requires that students sit in *seiza* from a standing position, sit for prolonged periods, and then stand from a sitting position.

Sitting in *seiza* is also about *shisei*, or a posture that exudes a feeling of dignity. Your posture is straight with a feeling of your head being pulled straight up from the crown. Like stretching the spine and lifting the head, you'll bring your ears directly over the shoulders. Your *metsuke* (gaze) should be cast slightly downward.

Steps to Sitting in Seiza

While there are minor variations as to how you get into position to sit in *seiza*, you'll generally begin by standing with your feet relatively close together.

Step slightly back with the left foot bending on the toes and kneeling down on the left knee. Similarly go back with the right foot bending on the toes and kneeling down on the right knee. Keep your upper body and shoulders straight, face forward and head up.

Your knees should be approximately two (2) hands width apart. The small of the back should be pressed slightly forward while resting your body weight forward onto the legs and knees, which shifts the weight off the ankles and allows you to sit more comfortably.

Flatten your feet with your toes down on the floor. Let your arms hang down from the shoulders with your elbows at the sides, and let your hands rest palms down approximately mid-thigh. Your fingers should be extended straight and angled slightly towards the inside of your legs.

Step 1

Step 2

Step 3

Step 4

Step 5

Step 6

Standing up is the reverse. Rise up on your toes first, bring your thighs and knees together, and extend first the right foot followed by the left as you stand. It's best to make this movement in a complete fluid motion.

Variations

There are stylistic variations that some consider important while seated in *seiza*. These descriptions of bowing show that deference and respect is extremely important to the martial approach in Aikido.

During Japan's feudal period, samurai would wear their swords on the left side, and draw the weapon using a leading right hand with a simultaneous forward movement of the right foot.

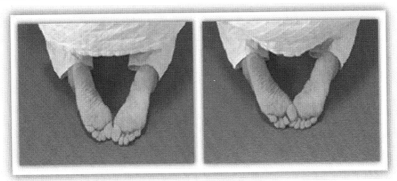

Some Aikidoka add placement of their left big toe on top of the right one (above) to demonstrate their respect by making a forward movement from that position a difficult feat.

Others cross their left foot over the right to further exaggerate this point. All methods are correct, provided you understand the reasons for the variation and thereby undertaking the practice.

Alternative Sitting Methods

Some people aren't able to sit in *seiza* for extended periods of time, so accommodations are made for them. The Aikido dojo usually makes no differentiation between the sexes, so both men and women may sit in a crossed-legged fashion.

Women have the added option of sitting with their legs to one side (which is exclusively female and follows Japanese social custom). However, men should only sit crossed-legged as is the custom for them.

There are rules to follow for these alternative positions. The bottom of your feet should never face the *shomen* or anyone else. Before using an alternative seating method, you should first sit in *seiza*, complete a seated bow, and then position yourself in crossed-legged seating. The bow signifies an apology for the disturbance.

Knee Walking (*Shikko*)

Walking on your knees (known as "samurai walk" or *shikko*") is part of Aikido due to its historical significance and practical training. Japan's feudal period etiquette is linked to the use of a sword and other weapon arts, as well as to strategies of self-defense and the ability to react instantaneously.

Warriors (*bushi*) were pledged to protect their nobility, and were bound by custom to sit in *seiza* in the presence of nobility. The *bushi* developed skills to move and engage in combat within these various constraints, and *shikko* movement was among these innovative measures.

In terms of practical training purposes, *shikko* helps you to study techniques and movements in greater detail. Another benefit is the strengthening of your legs, balance, proper hip movement and improving flexibility. Students develop a better center or balance while performing techniques without the use of their legs.

Certain training techniques require students to move while on their knees. *Hamni handachi* and *suwariwaza* require one or both participants to be on their knees throughout the entire technique.

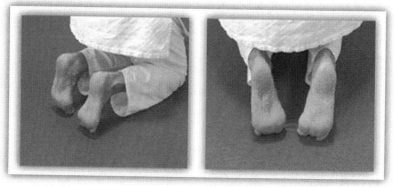

Starting in *seiza*, begin by raising your feet up into a toe stand position (*kiza*). Movement in any direction can be initiated from this position.

With practice, students develop the ability to move in all directions – backwards, forwards, sideways – to a complete 360-degree turn (the photos above illustrate the technique). As with most techniques, *shikko* is best learned from an experienced instructor.

The Line-Up

Every formal training class (*keiko*) begins and ends seated with the students in a straight line while in *seiza* facing the *shomen*. Once they're so aligned, they perform a bowing – in ceremony.

This seated line-up is usually formed following positions of rank. To figure out where your placement should be requires knowing which side of the room is designated the high side (*joseki*) and the lower side (*shimoseki*). This would be right to left (high to low) in most situations, but could be reversed due to the building's design.

Students sit in *seiza* from oldest to youngest in age within the rank, and then by the rank level. If two people are the same age and rank, the senior person is defined as the one who came to the dojo first. Every class has a different group of people attending, so a student's placement will vary during each session.

If a person is visiting the dojo, proper etiquette is for them to take a place below the most junior ranked individual regardless of their own rank.

When taking a place at the line-up, enough room between the students next to you needs to be left so that everyone can comfortably execute a seated bow.

A rule of thumb would be to extend your elbows out with your hands resting on your thighs, thereby allowing enough space between the person(s) next to you so you don't touch them. This amount of space between bodies provides a comfort zone.

If the class is a large group, more than one row may be needed and follows the same ranking etiquette previously described.

Once everyone is in place, there's usually a brief period of complete stillness. *Mokuso* (a time for meditation and reflection) is used to transition oneself from the outside world to a training mindset. The same is done at the end of the class to contemplate the training experience and transition back to the outside world.

The instructor initiates a group bow towards the *shomen*. At many dojos, there is also a symbolic clapping of hands. Upon straightening from the bow, everyone raises their hands above eye level and in position to clap. At the instructor's initiation, everyone simultaneously claps twice before making another seated bow.

The bows, directed to the *shomen*, symbolize respect for the spirit-principles of Aikido and its Founder, Morihei Ueshiba, for developing the system of study.

The instructor will next face the class and initiate another seated bow. At the beginning of class the instructor says *"onegai shimasu"* ("please receive my instruction in this way"). The same ceremony is repeated at the end of class where the instructor will say *"domo arigato gozaimashita"* ("thank you for accepting my instruction").

(As previously noted, Japanese expressions aren't always translated correctly in English or another language meaning; therefore words and phrasing needs to be understood based on situational circumstances. This is the case in the opening and closing phrases said by the instructor and students.)

The clapping of hands represents *musubi* or unity, and is an integral part of the ceremony and the rich spiritual heritage of Japan. These practices are not religious in nature, but symbolic of Aikido's *ki* or life force energy principle. The claps can signify the practitioner's *ki* energy being sent outward and then received back from the Universe.

One may place a personal and/or spiritual aspect to this act if they so wish; otherwise, it's purely symbolic of an essential Aikido principle. Some dojos do not practice this portion of the ceremony, so again when in Rome do as the Romans do.

The Class

Sensei will begin formal instruction to the class after the bowing-in ceremony, which often begins with a warm-up and *ki* development exercises.

Most verbal and demonstrations are given while the students are in the line-up position. Once the warm-up is concluded, students return to the line-up for further instruction.

Note that during class the line-up does not follow any particular ranking etiquette. However, students desiring to be used as *uke*, or want the best view of the *Sensei*, will often take a place in the middle or center of the line.

There are a few simple words that most instructors use while running a formal class: *Hajime* (begin or start) lets the students know they may start doing whatever was just demonstrated.

Instructors signal that they are ready to provide a demonstration with the verbal command *yamete* ("stop what you are doing"), or with a double clap of their hands, and often both simultaneously. Again, students respond by sitting in seiza at the line-up.

This brings up an important safety requirement. The instructor is responsible for the safe conduct and operation of the class. During class their word is law and students need to obey all their directions.

Nothing is more important than stopping "on a dime" when told to stop! As soon as you hear "*yamete*" or "*matte*" ("wait" or "hold on"), even if you are in mid-stride cease all movement lest you may injure or be injured by your partner.

The Formal Closing

The instructor signals the conclusion of class either verbally or with a double clap of their hands. All students will line up, as at the beginning of class. Then the bowing-out ceremony is the exact replica as at the start of the session.

A formal class usually concludes with a community circle. After the aforementioned bowing ceremony, the instructor will move to a place near the *shomen* before inviting everyone to join them.

Students form a semicircle around the *shomen* with the instructor at one end. It's important that no one has their back turned towards the *shomen* as this would be considered disrespectful.

Old school etiquette has the most senior ranked student seated next to the instructor, and everyone else sitting according to rank. A variation has Sensei seated across the highest ranked student and below the lowest ranked student.

This is often explained as a 'most humble' position for Sensei, and is reserved for their discretionary use. Most dojo instructors would not take this placement, as the vast majority of dojos have suspended nearly all formality. Instead, they will ask that everyone quickly form the semicircle regardless of their rank.

This is usually a time for announcements or updates on events. Once finished, there are two generally practiced conclusions to the *keiko*. The first method has the instructor once again bowing to the students and thanking them for their participation. Sensei will then stand and step out of the circle.

The next most senior student will bow and leave the circle, followed by the next closest ranked student and so forth. In this way, the instructor and each student makes a respectful bow to all the training partners together.

The second method is for the instructor to bow, thank the students, and ask them to do the same with each of their training partners individually. Instructors usually remain seated while the students pay their respects.

Students will locate everyone with whom they just trained, and make an individual seated bow to each one of them. Students will also make an individual seated bow to the instructor as part of this method.

Student Responsibilities

The students make the dojo a place to train; therefore, if there were no students there would not be a dojo. If no one provides instruction, the students would not have a dojo. Therefore, Sensei is as important to the dojo as are the students, and both are required for the dojo to exist.

Here's a twist on Eastern versus Western thinking. For lack of a better description the majority of Aikido dojos are not-for-profit operations, even when they aren't legally structured as a nonprofit organization.

I'm referring to the fact that most schools don't operate to make money. How's that for a socialist approach? Few, if any, instructors are able to make their living from teaching Aikido, so their choice to instruct or operate a dojo is usually a labor of love, which is both a wonderful and sad fact.

Although a person (*dojo cho*) or an organization owns the dojo, it's the students', instructor's and/or *dojo cho's* combined responsibility to keep the dojo in existence, so everyone has delineated roles to make sure it stays open and functioning well.

The physical maintenance of a dojo is the students' responsibility. Once class is concluded, students have certain tasks to complete, foremost of which is tidying the facility, and at a minimum sweeping or light cleaning. If the dojo is in a temporary location -- such as a hall or community room -- the mats and temporary *kamiza* need to be packed and put away, etc.

The saying "many hands makes for light work" is good to keep in mind. All students, regardless of their position within the dojo, are required to complete tasks that may take only a few minutes. These tasks also provide a student time to prepare to transition into the outside world by reflecting on things like the training they just received.

The students need to pay extra attention that Sensei is taken care of. As soon as possible after the end of class, someone (usually the student who received the most personal instruction during the class) needs to approach Sensei and help fold their *hakama*.

This is not only a sign of respect, but frees Sensei to do other more important things with their time.

The original Japanese approach required students to maintain living accommodations for their Sensei and family, which included ensuring adequate food supplies, clothing, and money for all their needs.

Live-in students, known as *uchi-deshi*, also did daily menial chores and took care of all of their Sensei's needs.

In today's world an arrangement such as this is rarely found. However, in keeping to the spirit of this traditional relationship, students need to make an effort to ease Sensei's burdens.

Symbolically this would mean to offer to undertake tasks that would free Sensei to do other things, or volunteer their time and talent along with other students when a major maintenance project is needed (i.e., a new coat of paint for the dojo, treat and oil the dojo weapons, etc.).

Students typically make a financial contribution in the form of monthly dues to help with dojo expenses in order to not burden Sensei with concerns of paying the bills.

While a new student isn't expected to participate much beyond the payment of dues and attending class, as time passes senior students have greater responsibilities and expectations.

Classroom Etiquette

Coming to Class

You should always strive to be punctual and be prepared for a training class. This means you need to be properly attired, stretched, warmed up, mentally alert and ready to fully participate.

Should you arrive late for class, don't allow your tardiness to interrupt the instructor or students. If you can't participate in the formal opening of the class, be quiet and politely wait for it to begin.

Once class has begun, wait for any instructions to be finished before bowing into the training area. Then sit in *seiza* near the edge of the mat until the instructor invites you to train.

The best location would be to sit towards the center edge to increase the likelihood the instructor will quickly see you. Make a formal seated bow once you're acknowledged, and join the group training.

Leaving During Class

If at any point you need to leave while class is still underway (such as in the case of an injury), make sure the instructor is aware you need to leave. This can be accomplished by saying "*sumimasen*" ("I am sorry for the interruption"), and briefly state why you must leave.

Not only is this courteous, but the instructor is charged with your safety and well-being during class. Therefore, they need to know if there has been an injury so that appropriate action can be taken.

If you know you'll need to leave prior to the end of class, speak with the instructor before class begins. They will decide whether it's acceptable for you to participate, or provide instructions as to how and when you may excuse yourself from the class.

Bowing and Respecting the Shomen

The best rule to follow when following bowing etiquette is "when in doubt bow." Showing respect to the dojo, your instructor and fellow students is always the correct thing to do.

You should always face the Shomen, and avoid turning your backside in that direction since doing so is considered disrespectful and rude. The exception is when you exercise in actual training during class. Otherwise, the only person permitted to have their back turned, out of necessity, is the instructor.

Respecting Your Fellow Students

Everyone attending class should be treated with equal respect regardless of their rank or position within the dojo. Following the bowing etiquette described earlier is only the beginning of demonstrating that respect.

In partnered exercises, both students reach an agreement to train together. In essence, they're agreeing to be responsible for the physical safety of each other, and to execute their roles in the exercise to the very best of their abilities.

Obviously the degree to which a student can fulfill those obligations is predicated by their individual skill level, so these general understandings are the manifestation of mutual respect.

Knowing how to interact with others at the dojo offers the road to successful training is covered in the next few chapters.

CHAPTER THREE

Honorifics and Titles

How to Address People

Westerners tend to refer to people with a gender-specific Mr., Mrs., Miss, or Ms., and sometimes will identify someone by their educational or position status and address them as Doctor or Professor. However, modern society seems to be moving away from almost all formality in everyday use since it's a rare occurrence when people use a title when addressing someone.

But that's not the case in the Japanese or dojo culture. Technically honorifics aren't part of basic Japanese grammar, but are very much a part of its sociolinguistics. Therefore, it's beneficial for someone training in any Japanese martial art to have a general understanding of grammar and social etiquette.

An honorific is generally used when referring to the person you're talking to or an unrelated third party, so dropping the honorific suffix is considered rude and arrogant. Using an honorific when referring to yourself is simply not done, and is also considered rude and arrogant.

There are many rules as to which form of an honorific should be used in appropriate Japanese speech. Honorifics can be used for both males and females. The most commonplace *san* is a title of respect typically used between equals of any age.

Derived from the more respectful *sama*, *san* is almost universally added to the end of a person's name. For example, when referring to someone named James, *san* is added to become James-san.

San is also used with a variety of objects or nouns, and can be added to an occupation, company or institution (a bookseller might be referred to as *honya–san* -- bookstore + san).

Sama is a more respectful version of *san*, as it's used to refer to people much higher in rank than you, your guests, and sometimes people you greatly admire.

Kun is used by persons of senior status in addressing or referring to those of junior status.

Common Honorifics Used in a Dojo:

- *Senpai* is used to address one who is a senior student to you.

- Though someone of equal or lower level than yourself is referred to as **kohai**, you would still address them with the honorific *san*.

- Like Doctor in English, *senpai* can be used by itself as well as with a name (i.e., Senpai Bob or Bob-Senpai. Due to the phonological rules of the Japanese language, although it's spelled with an "n" the word sounds like "m," thereby being pronounced *sempai*.)

- *Sensei* literally means "former born, or one who has gone before," and is used to address all teachers. Someone who instructs a class, regardless of their rank, is always addressed as *Sensei* during class.

- **Dan** ranks imply one's level of mastery of the art. Again, due to Japanese phonetics *dan* is pronounced "don." Holders of first, second and third *dan* ranks are referred to individually as *senpai*. Those ranked fourth *dan* and above are always addressed as *Sensei*.

The most senior level Aikido instructors are increasingly using the title *Shihan*, meaning "to be a model," which conveys respect as Master. One always addresses senior instructors as *Sensei*. You would not address someone as *Shihan* Bob in the first person, but may do so in the third person.

Additionally, there are certain titles frequently used to refer to the top person within the dojo or organization: *Cho, Kancho,* and *Soke* all generally translate into the "head of" or "top of." Therefore, the dojo *Cho* is the head of the dojo, while *Kancho* and *Soke* generally refer to the head of the organization.

CHAPTER FOUR

The Senpai and Kohai Relationship

The hierarchy within the dojo is Sensei is at the top, and teaches Aikido techniques, attitudes and so on. *Senpai* and *kohai* are *deshi* (students) of Sensei.

Sensei may have one or more students who are charged with providing formal instruction and conducting classes.

The relationship between *senpai* and *kohai* comes to the dojo from the mentoring system widely used in Japan. There can be great differences of the system's use from business, social, education and familial situations.

There are certain nuances that can be difficult for someone from a Western culture to comprehend. But generally *senpai* is roughly the equivalent of the Western concept of a mentor, while *kohai* is roughly equivalent to a protégé. However, the relationship between the two is not as strong a connection as these words mean in the West.

Traditionally the person with more experience is considered to be the more senior student regardless of age or rank. Another way of thinking about this is that *senpai* is usually "one who came before." Therefore, Sensei will also acknowledge others who are their *senpai* while maintaining a position as *kohai* to these people.

The arrangement is often described as a senior and junior relationship. This is usually based on the senior person having greater knowledge and more time experience doing something than the other person regardless of physical skills and ability.

Another nuance to the relationship is that once established it rarely, if ever, changes no matter how much time passes or one's rank is elevated.

The *senpai/kohai* relationship is more than just a matter of respect and etiquette, as the system works on a mutual responsibility to each other. *Senpai* has a responsibility to help their *kohai(s)*, which can take the form of demonstrating techniques under Sensei's guidance, and passing on valuable knowledge in terms of dojo practices, etiquette, and information and so forth.

The general concept of helping *kohai* achieve their potential -- such as a mentor would do for a protégé – is to teach them all that one knows. *Kohai* has an equally important responsibility to humbly listen, and put into practice the demonstrations, information and criticism received from their *senpai*. The "spirit" of this special relationship is governed by mutual respect and common courtesy.

Looking at the system within the dojo culture, everyone is at one time or another either *senpai* or *kohai*. This would include someone who's only attended a single class in relationship to someone having their first Aikido experience. While it would best be left for a more seasoned student to take the initiative, there can be no doubt that someone attending their second class has more knowledge than someone attending their first.

CHAPTER FIVE

The Aikido Dojo

The dojo is where students receive most of their formal training. After they become accustomed to the basics of training in their first few sessions, an awareness of the particulars of the dojo begins. This usually starts by inquiring into why certain things are placed in a particular location, and what they are for.

The dojo has a two-part physical and spiritual purpose: The physical building or room is a place to practice techniques like throwing training partners, rolling, weapons, *kata*, etc., which lends itself to having people treat it much like they would a gym.

This makes perfect sense, since practice for the most part is a physical activity.

But at a deeper level, training is about connecting with a person's spirit. The word "dojo" means a place to "study the way." In a broader sense, it's a place to search for enlightenment since the physical training is a method in which people become enlightened and spiritual beings.

Dojo Layout: Joza and Shimoza (front and back)

The dojo layout has a historical basis. At one time there were practical concerns for having Sensei placed in front, seniors on the right, and juniors on the left. This arrangement provided the teacher maximum protection in an era when the warrior's primary weapon was the sword, which was carried on the left side and used with the right hand leading.

The arrangement also shielded the teacher's instruction from unauthorized observers, since only selected and authorized students were to be given instruction.

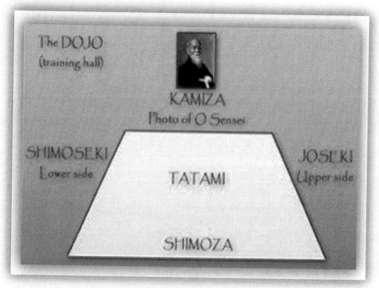

The dojo is arranged along the lines of a building designed in a complex matrix. The entrance is ideally opposite the *joza*, or the upper seat, and is sometimes called the *kamiza* (most Aikido dojos call this front wall the *shomen*).

Opposite is the *shimoza*, the lower seat (back wall), where the entrance is located. Facing the front to the right is the *joseki*, the upper side wall; and to the left is the *shimoseki*, lower side wall.

Seiki translates as "one's seat or place." The floor space where actual training takes place is referred to as *embujo* or *taijo*.

The training area typically has *tatami* mat flooring, which measure twice as long as they are wide. An Aikido dojo may have *tatami* made out of traditional material such as rice straw or compressed wood chips with a rush straw cover. These mats are then covered with a cloth fabric without any edging. Increasingly popular are mats made of synthetic, impact-dense materials since all flooring is designed to help lessen the impact of falls and rolls used in Aikido.

Many dojos are located in a shared space or part of a larger building; therefore, this aforementioned ideal design maybe adapted to suit the location.

The *shomen* or *kamiza* is immediately apparent due to a display of some kind being located there. There may be a *shiden* or elevated place here indicating a seat of honor, which is largely symbolic and reserved for paying respect to the Founder.

Other items such as a floral arrangement (*ikebana*), calligraphic scroll (*kakemono*), or a dojo banner (*hata*) can also be displayed. The arrangements can vary, but the general idea is to show that the *shomen* and its associated *kamiza* need to be considered the spiritual center of the room.

Most Aikido dojos today chose to de-emphasize some of the Japanese designs associated with a religious connotation. Instead, they opt to have a *tokonama* or display space located low to the ground in the *shomen*.

A rack of wooden tags identifying the ranks of the dojo members, or *nafuda kake*, can also be found on either of the side walls, although it's customary to be located on the *shimoza* (back wall). The side walls are usually reserved for weapon racks known as *doju kake*.

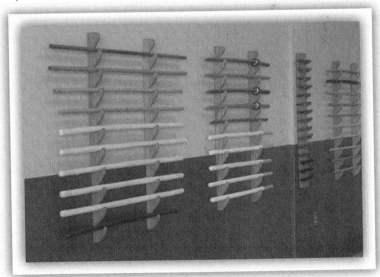

Everyone entering a dojo -- student or visitor alike -- completes a standing bow towards the *shomen* (front) on entering or leaving the dojo, because it is after all the spiritual center of the dojo.

Instructors typically seat themselves at the *joza* at the opening and closing of practice. Dojo members arrange themselves in order of seniority from *joseki* to *shimoseki* (right to left). Senior practitioners stay nearer the *joseki* (high side) when training, while juniors train on the *shimoseki* (low side).

Now that we've covered the basics of the dojo, it's time to get to your individual training – learning Aikido.

CHAPTER SIX

The Aikido Uniform

History of the Uniform

The *keikogi* (practice uniform) emerged during the late 19th century. Most people credit the founder of judo, Kano Jigoro, with the design of the modern-day uniform also known as a *dogi*. Gichin Funakoshi, the founder of Shotokan karate, is frequently credited for expanding the popular use of the *keikogi*. Up until the use of *dogi*, most martial arts did not have a specific uniform.

In English the *keikogi* is often referred to as *"gi,"* meaning clothes. Also, *keiko* is replaced with the name of the martial art being practiced. *Keiko* can also be replaced with *"do,"* which refers to the way -- meaning both the martial art and the lifestyle of the martial arts: *Aikidogi* (Aikido uniform), *Judogi* (judo uniform), *Kendogi* (kendo uniform), and so forth.

The *Aikidogi* has sleeves that stop just past the elbows, leaving the forearm and wrists unencumbered. The top part of the *keikogi* is called the *uwagi* (upper clothes), and the bottom is called the *shitabaki* (pants).

While *dogi* can be found in many colors, Aikido only uses the traditional white uniform. The third piece of the uniform is the *obi* or belt, which is wrapped twice around the waist and into a simple reef or square knot.

Today's *dogi* are constructed from various cotton and cotton-blended materials. The cloth weight of the *dogi* can range from a very light single to sturdy double weave materials, and all types can be found worn by Aikidoka.

How to Care for the Dogi

The condition of one's *keikogi* reflects on self-respect and self-discipline outside the dojo. It also suggests how one values their martial art and training partners.

A clean and serviceable *dogi* is a matter of health and safety. Washing your *dogi* by machine or hand is a preference. Use hot water and soap, but refrain from using bleach as it weakens the cotton fibers. Also, machine drying will shrink and stiffen the material. Hydrogen peroxide will remove blood stains (but be careful as stronger versions can also weaken fibers, so .08 strength is always good). Wearing a t-shirt or other undergarment will help absorb a lot of staining.

How to Fold the Dogi

Since the *keikogi* was only introduced in the late 19th century, there's no ancient ritual of *gi* folding. However, there are several efficient methods of folding that can transform the *dogi* into a small, easily carried package with smooth, clean edges.

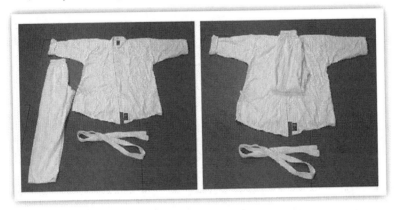

STEP 1   **STEP 2**

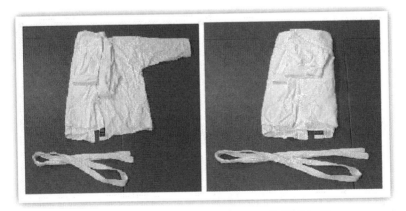

STEP 3   **STEP 4**

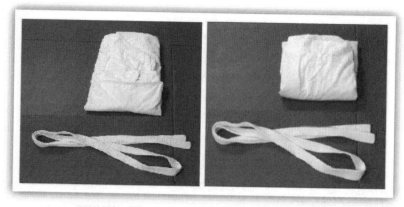

STEP 5

STEP 6

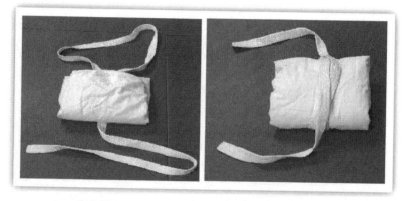

STEP 7

STEP 8

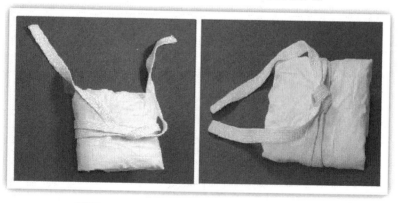

STEP 9

STEP 10

The Hakama

*'The hakama prompts us to reflect on the nature of true bushido.
Wearing it symbolizes traditions that have been passed down to us
from generation to generation. Aikido is born of the bushido spirit of
Japan, and in our practice we must strive to polish the seven
traditional virtues."* ~O'Sensei

One item of clothing that gets much attention between Aikidoka
is the *hakama*. The wearing of *hakama* visually sets Aikido apart
from the other martial arts who only wear *dogi*.

The *hakama* is training apparel with a direct connection to
Aikido's roots. Unlike the *dogi*, the hakama has a rich and varied
Japanese history. That history, relative to martial arts, finds that it
is rooted to the samurai horseman and archers of feudal system
Japan. It was meant to protect the rider's legs from brush, weeds,
chafing, etc., not unlike the Western cowboy's chaps.

Much like the cowboy versions, the *hakama* can be made from a variety of materials and fashioned into many styles, and some original versions were made from leather and later from cloth.

As an article of clothing the *hakama* developed into a fashion item throughout ancient Japan. It is still worn today in various formal styles designed for use on special occasions and at ceremonies.

There are variations to the design, with some formal *hakama* sewn as actual skirts without separate legs. Some are made of delicate silk, and others from sturdier materials worn in the martial arts. Beside Aikido, the *hakama* is used in the Kendo, Iaido, Kyudo, and Jujitsu martial arts.

The style worn by today's martial artist is called a *joba hakama*, which roughly translates into a horse-riding type of contraption you step into (the divided skirt makes straddling a horse easier).

For *Aikidoka*, the *hakama* is a combination training tool, symbol and reminder of the *budo* virtues handed down from O'Sensei.

The Founder had a rigid requirement that all who trained with him must wear the *hakama* regardless of age, rank or gender lest they arrive wearing only their *dogi* that in his day was considered an undergarment.

There are several stories that have suggested the meaning of the pleats in the *hakama* design. A typical *hakama* has four pleats on the right leg and three on the left.

However, there's no authentic historical Japanese text on clothing that supports the most commonly told story, at least in Western dojo.

Many Sensei explain the seven pleats on the front side of the *hakama*, each with their own symbolic meaning, using purported samurai values:

1. **Yuki** - courage, valor, bravery
2. **Jin** - humanity, charity, benevolence
3. **Gi** - justice, righteousness, integrity
4. **Rei** - etiquette, courtesy, civility (obedience)
5. **Makoto** - sincerity, honesty, reality
6. **Chugi** - loyalty, fidelity, devotion
7. **Meiyo** - honor, credit, glory, dignity, prestige

A more reasonable version of the different number of pleats that has a "martial" basis to it is where the sword is carried on the left hip.

Standing on the right leg at first meant less vulnerability to surprise attack. The less bulky right side made for easier and quicker movement of the right leg.

Both versions provide some historical context to the revered *hakama*.

A single pleat is on the back side of the *hakama* (see previous page). A traditional garment has a small spatula-shaped tab sewn to the top of this pleat -- a *hera*, meaning spatula – which is designed to be tucked into the back of the *obi* (belt) to help keep the waist of the *hakama* in place.

Besides knowing the history of the *hakama*, the next most frequently asked question is when can a *hakama* be worn?

The policies related to wearing a *hakama* in today's Aikido dojo began during post-World War II Japan when all *budo* activities enforced by the U.S. lead forces occupying Japan were suspended and there was a shortage of materials.

Aikido was among the few arts that was allowed to openly train, but care was taken to prevent undue attention to the martial aspects of the art. This de-emphasis on *budo* permeated Aikido for decades after the war, and is partially responsible for the art being labeled as "soft."

Due in part to the material shortage, many students fashioned their *hakama* from window curtains, futon covers, and a variety of fabrics which made for a very colorful dojo. Almost all of the *hakama* didn't last long due to cheap quality, dyes and poor material not conducive to hard training, which led to a decision to suspend the use of the *hakama*.

Later only *Yudansha* (black belts) could wear *hakama*. Women of *kyu* rank were allowed to wear the *hakama* earlier than men to preserve their modesty.

This historical background translates into many dojo adopting varied *hakama* policies today. It's not unusual to find that at one dojo only Yudansha (black belts) may wear a *hakama*, while at others everyone is encouraged to wear one.

Selecting an Aikido Hakama

Aikidoka wear a traditional black or indigo (dark blue) fabric *hakama*. As previously noted, the main body is constructed similar to pants in that it is divided into leggings.

The front has seven folds/pleats, giving the *hakama* the appearance of a skirt, and there are four *himo* (straps/cords). The front has a panel with two shorter straps attached, and there is a stiffened *koshiita* (back) with two longer *himo* (straps).

Hakama can be purchased from several sources, as well as being homemade by using sewing patterns. There are several types off the rack *hakama* from martial arts supply stores, mail order and Internet websites, and semi-custom made *hakama* are also available via online sources.

There are numerous things to consider when selecting a *hakama*. First you need to decide on the cut and style of the front and back panels which is a personal preference.

If you tie your *obi* (belt) so that it's parallel with your waist, you'll want a *hakama* that uses a straight front panel. However, if you tie your belt to align downwards from the waist, you'll want a *hakama* with an extended, longer front panel.

The *koshiita* (back) can be found in two common styles. The traditional style is cut at an angle, and has a flexible backing insert to provide support to the small of your back. This is the most common style used in Kendo, Iaido, and Jujitsu martial arts.

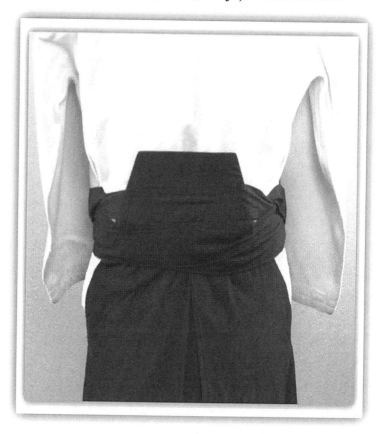

There's also a low-cut style of back known as an *aiki*. This softer *koshiita* is well suited for the types of *ukemi* (falls/rolls) in Aikido. Again, this is personal preference.

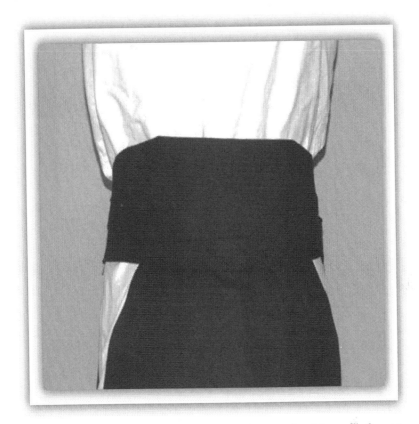

Aikidoka wear *hakama* as a training tool with one function being to help with their footwork. Another is to wear proper *budo* attire. Since having the correct length *hakama* is extremely important, it should be sufficient to cover the legs down to the top (break) of the foot.

Just as you wouldn't wear pants that were several inches too short and revealed your socks, the *hakama* should be long enough to not expose bare legs.

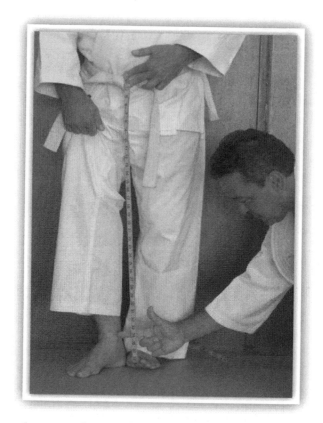

A good way to determine the proper length while hemming a *hakama* is to have someone help you with measurements. While wearing your *dogi/gi* (uniform) hold a cloth tape measure above the knot of your *obi* with one hand. Using your other hand hold the tape in at your waist, then run it over the knot of your *obi* and bring it in again at the bottom of the knot. Let the tape fall, have your helper note the measurement, then order the *hakama* according to this specific length (see type of material information below).

If your style preference is to tuck the *hakama* over the *obi* with an extended front panel, then tuck the tape measure in about one to two inches as you would the *hakama*. Round this measurement up to the nearest inch, and shop for a *hakama* made to that length.

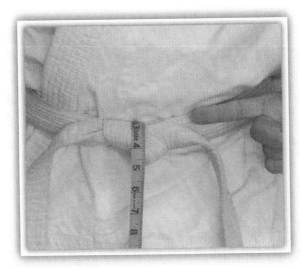

If you get an off-the-rack *hakama* or it needs altering, before it's hemmed keep in mind the type of fabric it's made of to determine if there will be shrinkage from cleaning. Traditionally, people hand wash their *hakama*. But some people dry clean it, in which case there will be little to no shrinkage (remember, dry cleaning solutions can break the fabric down over time).

Unless the fabric is 100% polyester, washing can shrink the garment. So before hemming add at least one to two inches or more to its length, depending on the content of the material before hemming allows for shrinkage. If there any doubts, consult the manufacturer before cutting anything off. Typical fabrics range from lightweight synthetics and cotton-polyester blends to 100% cotton.

The climate where you train will likely determine the fabric that works best for your *hakama*. Warmer climates bode well for a lighter material, and cooler climates might require a heavier material. Many Aikidoka who travel frequently have a second lightweight *hakama* to take to seminars for their convenience, and train at home with a more durable *hakama*.

How to Wear a Hakama

Although there are many ways to tie the *hakama* on yourself, it's best to have your Sensei or a trusted Senpai (senior student) show you how to tie it according to your dojo's customs. There are many nuances in Japan regarding the tying of knots and bows. The culture places a great deal of significance on the different ways to tie things together and nowhere is more significant than the wearing of the hakama.

Following is one of the generally accepted ways of tying on the Aikido *hakama.* First, the *himo* (cords) are wrapped around and through the *obi* (belt) that is tied into a simple square or reef knot.

Most Aikidoka tie the *obi* knot in front; however, the knot is traditionally tied in the rear to serve like a bustle (especially for ceremonial wear), and hikes the back of the *hakama* up just enough so that it doesn't drag on the ground or get in the way of one's heels.

The longer set of *himo* are wrapped and then tucked inside the *hakama* underneath the *obi*. The shorter *himo* are then wrapped and tied on the outside of the *hakama* usually into a bow on the front.

Again, there are numerous methods and styles to tying on a *hakama*, so you'll need to learn the style preferred at your dojo.

How to Care for a Hakama

Great care and respect should be given to your *hakama*, which should be laundered separately from other clothing. It must be properly folded and stored, and shouldn't be bundled and tossed into a carry bag as though it was dirty laundry.

In terms of laundering the hakama, most Aikidoka hand wash it using cold water and mild detergent, then hang and air dry -- often pinning the pleats to help keep them in form. A final step would include a light ironing of the pleats.

However, there are some who drop the hakama off at the dry cleaners (finding a cleaner that can properly press the pleats can be chore unto itself). Therefore, the best way to maintain crisp, neat pleats is to properly fold and store your hakama.

How to Properly Fold a Hakama

There's a proper method to folding the *hakama* into a neat package that keeps the pleats in place and makes for easy carrying.

Folding the *hakama* at first can be a little frustrating. With some practice it becomes routine and is usually completed in a few minutes.

The time set aside at the end of class for folding the *hakama* also provides an opportunity to reflect and prepare for the transition to the outside world.

Begin by lying the *hakama* on the floor with its back side facing up. Straighten the two leggings and evenly crease them into the center. (Some people find it easier to hold the *hakama* while standing with the *koshiita* tucked under their chin to straighten this initial fold.)

This first step is <u>critical</u> to successfully completing all the other folding tasks.

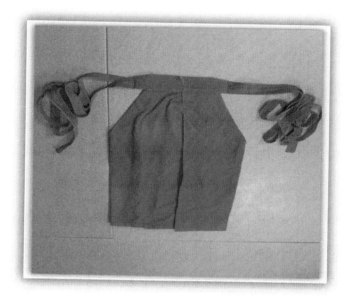

Holding the ends of the *hakama* with either hand, flip it over so that the pleated front side is facing up. Then straighten the pleats and smooth out the fabric.

Take one side and fold it toward the center to cover one-half of the pleats (above), then do the same with the other side (below).

Determine where to fold the length so you can make four quarter sections. Fold this first section and check that the back crease is even.

If at any time during this process the crease is misaligned, unfold the *hakama* and start the process over.

Once folded into fourths, use the *himo* to tie up the package. Remember, the Japanese place great significance on tying things in a certain way, so begin with the two longest *himo* and fold them onto themselves by half, then fold over again.

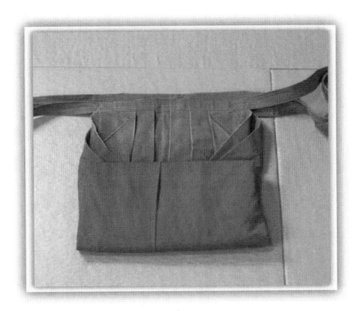

Carefully lay the *himo* across each other; then take the two shorter ones and loop them around and back out underneath so that the ends are sticking straight up. Then do the same to the other side.

Finally, fold the remaining lengths onto themselves, and neatly tuck the ends under the loop that has been formed.

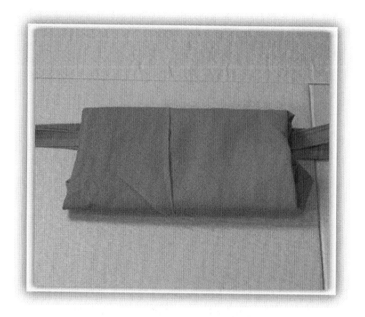

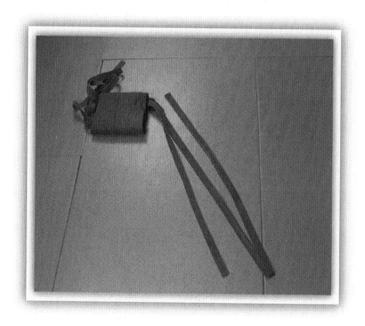

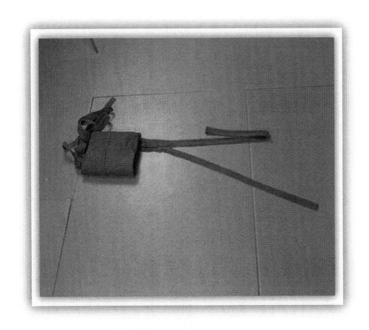

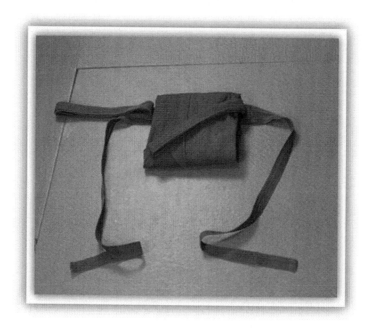

CHAPTER SEVEN

Aikido Weapons

Aikido is deeply rooted in the ancient Japanese combat methods. Archery, spear, sword and other battlefield techniques form the basis of many of its movements. Today's dojo design, décor and use of certain apparel by practitioners are symbolic of their original purpose.

The *dogu* (tools) are specific to each martial art. Aikidoka use wooden training weapons that maintains a connection to these warrior roots.

There are only a few frequently used training weapons in Aikido (style and training curriculum varies among dojo instructors, so not all of the weapons mentioned here may be used). Aikido uses special versions of these martial arts weapons, so you need to be certain to get the proper version for your Sensei's style.

Standard weapons are generally made of Japanese white oak or impact grade hickory, which are readily available and reasonably priced. They're carefully selected for their impact strength and density to make a training instrument that will hold up during frequent use.

Some equate the Japanese white oak with the same reverence a baseball player might give to a hickory baseball bat as it is considered an "old school" traditional standard.

There are also a number of exotic woods and composite materials available today. Like the titanium baseball bat versus an old hickory bat, these materials are stronger and longer lasting than standard wood materials.

You should be cautious of using weapons made from these materials during regular training as safety is of paramount importance. Selecting the correct material for your training weapons should be consistent with the type of equipment your training partners use. You wouldn't want to train with a weapon so hard and tough that it damages your partner's training weapon. Splintering or a total failure of a wooden weapon poses a serious safety issue for everyone.

If you're new to training with weapons, consult your Sensei or one of the senior students at your dojo for guidance as they can best provide information on the appropriate size, material and style of weapons used at your dojo.

These elements significantly impact your training experience, since a weapon that is extra long, too thick or heavy would not be welcome in class.

It's been my experience that Aikido students either love or hate weapons training. I'm one of the latter and would avoid these classes whenever possible. Admittedly I am hand – eye – feet coordination-challenged. Much to my parent's chagrin, years of formal dance lessons during my formative years never helped their gawky kid develop graceful coordination or movements. However, today they'd be proud to see me move on the training mat.

Weaponry and Eye-Hand Coordination

If you're among the well-coordinated people who love picking up a wooden stick and easily maneuvering and adapting to new forms and kata, you're a step ahead of the Aikido learning curve.

Sooner or later most Aikidoka come to realize that weapons training is essential. I struggled for years until a very patient instructor sat me down and gave me the cold hard facts.

He said I had to develop weapons skills if I wanted my open hand techniques to improve and be effective. There you have it! So now I embrace every opportunity to attend weapons class, though I'm still among the slower students to pick up new movements.

Weapons training is either about sticking to precise repetitive movement or creatively responding to situational attack. To develop those necessary skills you'll require the use of some special tools. And like anything special, you'll need to treat those tools with care and respect.

Jo Short Staff

The *jo* staff is a versatile training weapon, and its design and ability to disable an opponent has remained unchanged for over 400 years. It's used in many martial arts, and is found in all sorts of sizes, diameters and tapers.

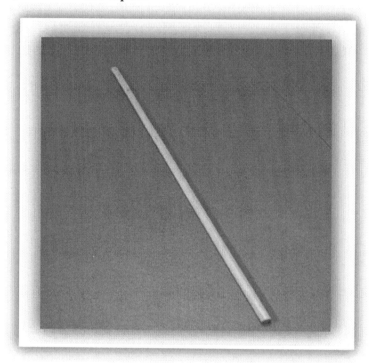

Jo techniques can be generally described as sliding movements through the practitioner's hands to strike, punch or deliver a blow to an opponent.

How to Select a Jo Staff

Aikido training utilizes a straight staff approximately 7/8" round (2.22cm) and 50-54" (127-137 cm) in length.

To determine the proper length for your *jo* staff, stand very straight and have a helper take a measurement from the ground up to the underarm.

Customizing a *jo* may require cutting some length off a longer stick and refinishing the wood (see how to maintain wood weapons).

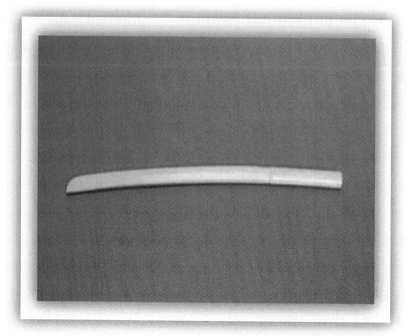

Bokken

The *bokken* is fundamental to Aikido's swordsmanship heritage, and is used in various martial arts. The Aikiken version is a wooden sword of medium weight and diameter, and is well-balanced with a curvature and proportion of a real sword (*katana*).

Its purpose during training is to facilitate movement and skill rather than to imitate use of an actual sword. Practice is usually paired with a partner. However, movement is founded on a "live blade" concept by treating the *bokken* as though it were a real cutting blade.

A typical *bokken* is 40-42" (100-106 cm) in overall length, and the design has several sections from tip to butt end. The butt end of the handle is sometimes tapered smaller to accommodate the palm and is a stylistic option.

The Aikiken is usually squared off into a blunt point 1 to 2 inches (2.5 to 5cm) long, but certain styles can be rounded or pointed.

The blade section is slightly curved like a real sword 26 to 29 inches (66 to 74 cm) in length, and the average length of this section is between 9 to 11 inches (23 to 28 cm).

The handle or hilt is flat, and depending on personal preference may include having a notch carved at the top section. The notch is designed for use of a guard (*tsuba*), which is removable and held in place using a rubber grommet. Guards can be made of plastic, leather or wood.

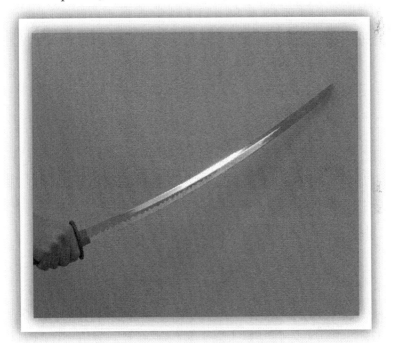

Aikido styles that don't affix a guard use a *bokken* with a smooth transition into the handle. The guard on a real sword is present to prevent the user's hand from sliding up onto the cutting edge of the blade. It also protects the user's hands in an Aikiken from blows and strikes.

How to Design a Custom Bokken

Bokken are normally made to a general size standard. However, to truly get a proper fit for one's height and grip, a custom weapon can be made. A custom Aikiken, using either Japanese white oak or impact grade hickory, is only slightly more expensive than a standard *bokken*. It does require waiting time, since most craftsmen who make these items usually have a long list of orders. But many consider the extra cost and wait well worth it.

Measuring the specifics for a *bokken* is required regardless of the material choice, so you'll begin by deciding the "blade" length. If a standard *bokken* is available, use it as a guidance tool; otherwise, any type of long stick will suffice.

Stand erect with both hands at your side, and hold the *bokken* or stick in your right hand. Relax and allow your hand to sink down slightly while allowing the *bokken* or stick to slide through your grip. Marking where your grip ends and measuring the distance to the ground will provide the approximate blade length.

Next, determine the length of the handle. There are two common methods to measure this factor, so use either one or an average of both:

1. The first method, known as the three-hand method, is to grip your sample *bokken* or stick with the butt end in the fleshy part of your left hand.

Place your right hand on the *bokken* immediately in front of your left hand; then release your left hand and place it immediately in front of your right hand. Mark and measure the distance from the butt end.

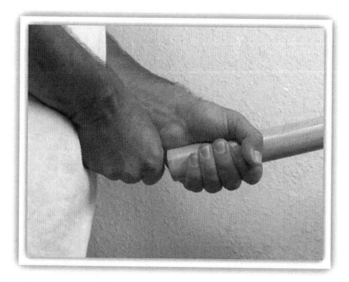

2. The alternate method is to take the *bokken* in your left hand with butt end firmly in the meaty part of the palm. Ball your right hand into a fist, and place it at your mid-section (at the belly button). Bring the *bokken* that's held in your left hand even to the fist. Release your right hand and raise it towards your head with a relaxed bend at the elbow; then lower your right hand and place it comfortably on top of the handle. Mark and measure the distance to the butt end.

The Bokken Style

As previously noted, your Sensei's training style will dictate the form of the *bokken's* tip, curvature and whether or not it uses a guard. So the final decision to make will be the style of *bokken* you'll want to have.

Other Common Training Tools

The *jo* staff and *bokken* are the most frequently used weapons in Aikido, but there are several other training aids often used by instructors.

Shoto

Representing a *wakizashi* (side inserted sword) known as the samurai's short sword, the *Shoto* is usually made of impact-dense wood similar to the *bokken*. An average length is 24" (61 cm), but can also be found as short as 12" (31 cm). The variation in size is somewhere between the long sword and knife.

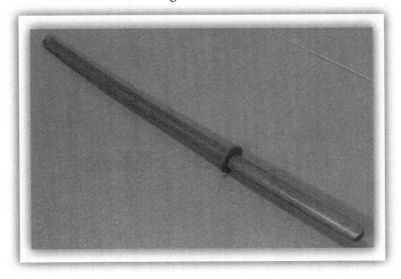

Hanbo or Tanto

Representing a knife, the *hanbo* or *tanto* is usually made of wood similar to the *bokken*. However knife like tools can be made of plastic or dull metal blades to help with realism in training. They can be found in all sorts of shapes and sizes. The average size ranges from 8-10" (20-25.4 cm).

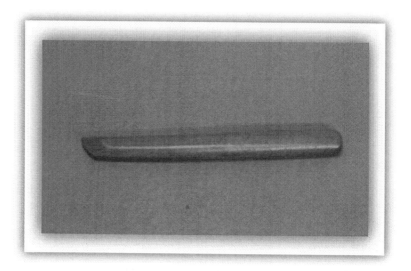

Suburitō

A *suburitō* is made of wood, but is longer and heavier than the *bokken*. Used as an individual training aid, a practitioner utilizes striking and cutting motions to build strength, stamina and speed. This type of training tool focuses on improvement with Aikiken movement.

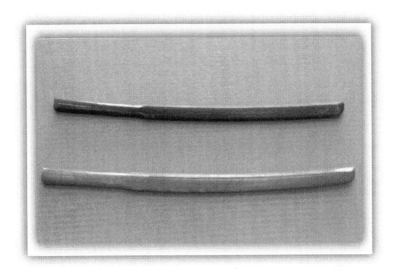

Shinai Take

The *Shinai Take* (flexible bamboo) is most often used in Kendo; however, a short version known as a *Fujuro Shinai* measures approximately 40" (102 cm) and is used in Aikido practice.

It's constructed from a divided staved cane section of bamboo, then covered with either cloth or protective leather. Its design allows users to practice sword techniques, and make physical contact without serious injury to training partners.

How to Care for a Wood Training Weapon

First, you need to know what type of wood the weapon is made from. Most weapons are constructed from Japanese white oak or impact grade hickory. But there are weapons made of exotic materials like Brazilian teak, cocobolo, rosewood, purple-heart, ebony, and composites.

The basic maintenance is the same for all wooden training aides (*jo* staff, *bokken*, or *tanto*); however, you may wish to finish them differently based on their intended use.

All materials described in the following instructions are readily available at most hardware and home improvement stores, and can be found in small and large quantities at a reasonable price.

Before you begin, carefully examine the wood. Shallow dings and dents from normal training are to be expected, and can be handled through a simple refinishing process.

A more skilled wood craftsperson should handle major damages like deep splintering or gouges found in the wood (this would be the exception rather than the rule).

Sanding

Begin by smoothing scratches and dents using medium grit sand paper and a sanding block if necessary; then follow this with a second pass using a fine grit paper. If you want to be really fastidious, you can finish with a super fine sanding to make it perfect. Wipe the wood with a clean cloth or paper towel before completing the refinishing process with an oiling.

Oiling

Boiled linseed oil is the most commonly used finish. A *jo* staff is designed to easily slide through the hands, so mix a small amount of mineral spirits into the oil which will dry to a smooth, slippery feel.

The *bokken* is designed to be gripped during use. Mix ten parts linseed and two parts tung oil together to create a "sticky grip" on the wood while your hands warm the oil during training.

Using a clean soft rag, begin by dabbing the weapon's ends with the oil that will allow for deep penetration. Then liberally wipe the entire weapon, let it set for approximately 10 minutes, and wipe off the excess oil with a clean rag. Depending on your climate, ambient temperature and humidity, the wood may take several days to fully dry. Make sure you have it in an area where there's no dust or anything that can stick to the oil.

Although other types of oil and wax can be used on wood weapons, the aforementioned procedure is widely used and very effective.

Remember to follow safe work habits by wearing eye and face protection. Oils are flammable so dispose of rags appropriately, and keep liquids away from anything that might ignite them.

Storage

If you use your weapons often (as you should), it's recommended that you keep them in a weapons bag. Store *bokken* with the handle end down. If they're left dormant for extended periods, lay them flat and out of extreme temperature changes.

Alternatively, there are inexpensive weapons racks that can be installed in your home. They serve both as a good way to store your weapons, and are an attractive decoration.

The Methodology of Weapon Handling

Handling bladed tools, like a *katana* (which is drawn from the left side using a leading right-hand) is to be mindful of how the weapon is designed to inflict injury. For example, the Aikiken (*bokken*) imitates the *katana*, and is designed to slice/cut an opponent.

Therefore classroom etiquette calls for the *bokken* to be placed either ready for use, as in paired practice, or politely in a safe position to indicate deference. The latter would be so that the handle/hilt is pointed left with the cutting edge towards the body so the weapon can't be easily used.

In this fashion the cutting edge is pointed towards the least threatening direction, which can vary depending on the situation (the following examples will help make this concept clearer).

Start and End of Class

At the beginning of class, bowing with a weapon should be done with the utmost submissiveness and respect for the instructor and other students. Have the weapon on your right side. If the weapon is a *bokken* or *tanto*, have the cutting edge of the blade turned towards your body.

Historically, samurai (aka: *bushi* or *buke*) would carry their swords on their left side with the blade's cutting edge facing upwards in a sheath and drawn forward with the edge facing away from the body.

Placing the weapon on your right side makes it more difficult to use, and therefore demonstrates greater deference.

Once class has begun the weapon should be held ready, mindfully and respectfully on your left side until the end of practice when the bowing ritual is repeated.

Handling a Weapon Exchange

You should treat the handling of the weapon by keeping the threat to personal safety and a martial spirit uppermost in thought. The following are considered safe positions in order to exchange a weapon with a training partner:

The hand-off begins with a respectful, slight standing bow of an approximate 15-degree angle while keeping your eyes focused on your partner. The person receiving the weapon accepts the weapon by placing their hands in a position that is least threatening for immediate use.

A *jo* staff is safest to use during a hand-off when it's in the neutral horizontal position while being held in both hands.

An edged tool (*bokken* or *tanto*) is safest during hand-off when it's positioned with the cutting edge away from your body, its tip angled towards your partner, and the handle/hilt closest to yourself.

In both situations, the weapon's position offers your partner the least likelihood of immediately using the weapon offensively.

Bowing with a Weapon

Aikido training uses weapons crafted from wood, which typically are the *jo staff* and *bokken*.

Standing Bow

Start by demonstrating respect for the weapon, and that it's available for use. Before stepping into the training area hold the weapon in both hands, raise it just above eye level, and complete a standing bow towards the *shomen* which signifies respect and gratitude. Then proceed to train.

Seated Bow

Bowing with a weapon is all about deference and respect. The most submissive position for a weapon placement when completing a seated bow would be directly in front of you.

The cutting edge of the blade (if there is one) faces towards you, and the handle (if present) is on the left.

This position would be the most difficult to be in to make an offensive move. In this instance, the offensive use is more difficult for you than for those in front (Sensei) or around you.

While the aforementioned position is the most deferential placement for a weapon, there is usually insufficient space in most dojo environments to use this placement.

The next best location is to place the weapon on the right side with the cutting edge facing towards you, which poses a lesser threat to anyone around you.

CHAPTER EIGHT

Aikido's Official Organization

Moriehi Ueshiba – Founder of Aikido (1883 – 1969)

Aikido is an international martial art, and is practiced in over 100 countries worldwide.

The expansion of Aikido between 1942 and 1980 can be largely credited to the post-World War II generation students of O'Sensei.

Kisshmoru Ueshiba (1921 – 1999)

Gozo Shioda (1915 – 1994)

Kenji Tomiki (1900-1979)

Minoru Mochizuki (1907-2003)

Kochi Tohei (1920-2011)

While many outstanding instructors left Japan to spread Aikido worldwide, there were key men including the founder's son, Kisshomaru Ueshiba; Goza Shioda; Kenji Tomiki; Minoru Mochizuki and Koichi Tohei who began their instruction during varying times of O'Sensei's life, which resulted in stylistic differences among this iconic generation of instructors. However, all of them maintained a core basis of the Aikido taught by the Founder. These divergences might be more properly called "sub-styles" of Aikido, and resulted in the creation of several governing organizations that constitute Aikido today.

Organizational structure helps coordinate standardized grading requirements and instructor titles. These organizations also bring a legitimizing aspect to the teaching of Aikido. This is not to imply that an instructor or dojo that has chosen not to align with an organization is not teaching real Aikido; rather, the choice of affiliation or non-affiliation is both a dojo financial operation and philosophical decision.

The original school of Aikido is the Aikikai, which is represented globally through the International Aikido Federation, the largest organization in the world.

Also known as the Aikido World Headquarters located in Tokyo, Japan, it has always been headed by the living successor of the Founder (Morihei Ueshiba) referred to as *Doshu*. This organization operates both the *Honbu* and *Iwama* dojo. People often refer to this organization simply as *Honbu* (phonetically pronounced Hom-bu).

As previously noted, there are other organizations and sub-styles that can trace their lineage through senior students back to the Founder, O'Sensei. After his death in 1969, more senior students branched out on their own to establish independent schools.

This trend continues today, with senior students of the senior students of O'Sensei coming to prominence in their own right. As of this writing, following are the major organizations other than the Aikikai:

Organization	Founder	Established	Commentary
Yoseikan Aikido	Minoru Mochizuki	1931	First Deshi to receive a license to establish his own ryu. Style incorporates judo and Aikido techniques.
Yoshinkan Aikido	Gozo Shioda	1955	Considered a "hard" style based on Aikijujutsu. Ki principles are de-emphasized.
Shin'ei Taido	Noriaki Inoue	1955	Originally called Shinwa Taido. Inoue was a nephew of O'Sensei and is closely associated with developing Aikibudo.
Shodokan Aikido	Kenji Tomiki	1967	Also known informally as Tomiki ryu, it includes a rule-based competition resulting in some calling it "sport Aikido." Emphasis on randori or multiple person attack, and individual kata.
Ki Society	Kochi Tohei	1974	Originally formed as Shin Shin Toitsu Aikido by Tohei (former head instructor at Honbu dojo) after political differences with the Doshu created a split from the Aikikai. Primary focus on Ki development.
Wadokai Aikido	Roy Suenaka	1975	Also known as Suenak-ha Tetsugaku-ho. Suenaka was a direct student of O'Sensei. The style blends technique and spiritualism of Aikido.
Fugakukai International Association	Karl Geis	1982	A branch split from Shodokan Aikido without the competition element. Combines judo, jodo and Aikido techniques.
Keijutsukai Aikido	Thomas H. Maikyama	1980	American born martial artist and senior Yoshikan student established a style focused on military and law enforcement technique use.
Kokikai Aikido	Shuji Maruyama	1986	Techniques de-emphasis on "hard" applications. Promotes minimum effort for maximum effect.
Yoshokai	Takashi Kushida	1991	A branch split by a former senior instructor of Yoshikan Aikido.
Nippon Kan	Gaku Homma	1978	Based in Colorado, USA, focuses on Iwama style technique, community support, and humanitarian works.
Shinshin Aikishuren Kai	Hitohiro Saito	2004	Split from Iwama ryu (Takemusu Aikido Kyokai) after Morihiro Saito's passing (2002).

Rank System(s)

The martial arts have traditionally used competition as a method to determine one's ability and position within the art. Aikido is an exception to this approach, as it is a non-competition *budo* (with the exception of Shodokan Aikido aka Tomiki Ryu). As such, individuals are ranked based either on an examination of prescribed technical requirements, or at much higher levels on their overall contributions to the art.

The *dan* (pronounce "don") ranking system is a Japanese mark of level, and translates as "step" or "stage." While the system has been around since the Edo period (17th century) of Japan, Kano Jigoro (the founder of Judo) is credited with incorporating it into the martial arts. *Dan* rank is used along with the lower grading system, *kyu* grade, in Aikido.

The different levels are typically identified with the wearing of colored belts (*obi*). A *dan* rank is signified with a black belt, while *kyu* grades are typically identified with the wearing of a white or colored *obi* other than black.

Kyu ranks progress using a descending order system, so first *kyu* is the highest. For example, the first *kyu* outranks second *kyu*. The *dan* ranking system starts after first *kyu*. Essentially, the *kyu* is the number of steps before reaching mastery, whereas the *dan* gives steps into mastery:

Grade	Pronunciation	Belt Color
6th Kyu	Rokkyu	White
5th Kyu	Gokyu	White
4th Kyu	Yonkyu	White or Blue
3rd Kyu	Sankyu	White, Blue or Brown
2nd Kyu	Nikyu	White or Brown
1st Kyu	Ikkyu	White or Brown

The generally accepted *dan* levels are 1 to 10. The highest levels of most martial arts, including Aikido, are reserved for the founder or leaders of the style:

Degree	Pronunciation
1st Dan	Shodan or Ichidan
2nd Dan	Nidan
3rd Dan	Sandan
4th Dan	Yodan
5th Dan	Godan
6th Dan	Rokudan
7th Dan	Shicihidan or Nanadan
8th Dan	Hachidan
9th Dan	Kudan
10th Dan	Judan

Lower *dan* grades are typically validated based on knowledge and physical skill. Holding a *dan* rank doesn't necessarily make one an expert; instead, it indicates the student is no longer considered a beginner, and possesses a certain degree of competence across a reasonable range of techniques. Lower *dan* levels can be awarded through an examination conducted by an authorized higher graded individual.

Higher *dan* ranks are awarded based on demonstrated leadership ability, teaching experience, and contribution to the art. A committee awards the upper *dan* levels after a review of the individual's qualifications.

Organizations have slightly varying approaches to the above rank system. The most common differences appear within the *kyu* grade practices. For example, some organizations have an affiliate-wide policy, and others allow individual dojo discretion to occur in *kyu* grading.

A generally seen approach to *kyu* rank designation is that each *kyu* is awarded a different color belt, ranging from white at sixth *kyu* to brown at first *kyu*. Others have a two or three color system beginning with white for sixth, fifth and fourth *kyu*; then graduating to blue or brown for third, second and first *kyu*. The wearing of a *hakama* may also be based on rank depending on the organization's policy.

Aikido for kids is among the fastest growing areas of Aikido today. However, since youth grading is not officially recognized by most of the major organizations, it's left to the discretion of the dojo *cho* (head of dojo).

Youth ranking often has many levels to help encourage, reward and promote interest among children. Many dojos adopt the Japanese academic *kyu* grading system for youth, which includes a pre-first and second *kyu* due to the difficulty in attaining first and second *kyu* levels. This may be followed by "junior" dan ranking.

The following table lists the standard academic grades:

Grade	Pronunciation
Non-grade	Mukyu
10th	Jikkyu / Jukkyu
9th	Kyukyu
8th	Hakkyu / Hachikyu
7th	Nankyu
6th	Rokkyu
5th	Gokyu
4th	Yonkyu
3rd	Sankyu
Pre 2nd	Jun-Nikyu
2nd	Nikyu
Pre 1st	Jun-Ikkyu
1st (Highest)	Ikkyu

Ranks and Titles

All instructors, regardless of rank grading, are referred to as "*Sensei*," and students are "*Deshi*." *Kyu* level students are known as *Mudansha* or *Kyudansha* (both names are used interchangeably in an English speaking dojo). Those without any ranking are more correctly referred to as *mudansha* (*mukyu* meaning "non-grade", and *kyu* meaning "without").

These individuals are considered as initiates rather than students, until they reach the first-degree black belt. The holder of a black belt of any degree is referred to as *yudansha*, or one with a *dan* grade.

Those who hold a first, second or third *dan* rank have reached a position where they are considered *fuku-shidon* (instructor assistant). Those who possess a fourth or fifth *dan* rank have reached a position of *Shidon* (instructor).

Holders of a sixth *dan* and above are considered *Shihan* (master instructor). All instructor levels are referred to as *Sensei*.

In addition, there are two other titles of importance: O'Sensei (great teacher) is reserved for Morihei Ueshiba, the Founder of Aikido. *Doshu* (head heir) is the title designated for the Founder's successor within the Aikikai.

The other organizations beside the Aikikai reserve a title for the founders of their individual *ryu* (school style). Typically they are referred to as *Kancho* or *Soke - Sousu* (head of the organization).

Examination Etiquette

Examination day is a momentous and happy occasion. While the person up for ranking is usually a bit anxious about having the spotlight shining on them, exams offer you an opportunity to be recognized for your hard work and skills. It's also a time for student and instructor to reflect on the progress made since the last exam.

You don't need to worry about meeting anyone's expectation level other than your own and Sensei's. Everyone is judged on individual merit, which is a wonderful aspect of Aikido as you're not expected to meet or exceed someone else. There's no direct competition; therefore, you're required to perform the specific techniques and demonstrate the skills appropriate for the rank level being sought.

Examinations are held at specific time intervals. *Kyu* exams are held several times each year as the time requirements are shorter than *dan* grades. Formal exams follow specific guidelines and etiquette. While the details of each exam will vary depending on the administrator and the grade being evaluated, the formal etiquette at examinations is held to a relative standard.

A fact often overlooked during an examination is that everyone in attendance is being observed and evaluated, so the individual being put through their proficiency is not alone. Those who are selected to help in the exam as *uke* (the attacking partner) are being observed as to their ability to properly follow directions and make a sincere effort. Those observing the exam are noted for how they adhere to proper dojo etiquette and attention.

Examinations follow a specific etiquette and order of activity. Some administrators consider proper etiquette as being more important than proficient technique.

Kyu level exams are prescribed in almost every way. Techniques, skills, etc., are published and known within the dojo, so there are few surprises during a *kyu* level exam.

Administrators may differ in how they conduct the exam; however, it's the responsibility of the person up for grading to arrange the partners for the exam.

It's often wise to enlist at least two (2) people to help as it ensures an adequate number of *uke* available in the event of illness or injury. Whenever possible, select someone of a higher rank than is being sought, as they will have already completed the exam requirements and will be capable of taking the appropriate *ukemi*.

Examination Partner

Being part of an exam is a valuable training opportunity. Since it's an honor and responsibility to assist in an examination, the exam partner's role is to be an aide to their partner (success or failure rides on clearly understanding this distinction).

An exam partner's role is to deliver the requested movement by the administrator with clear commitment and intention, regardless of the movement's speed needed for the skill level of the person being tested.

Some of the don'ts for an exam partner include second-guessing their partner's movement or to show openings (unless specified by the test administrator), or challenging their candidate in any way. Nor is it their place to fall for the candidate, or do any movements for them.

Traditionally, *Yudanshas* (*dan* ranks) serve on *dan* exams, and *Mudanshas* (*kyu* ranks) serve on *kyu* level exams. This follows standard dojo etiquette, unless the administrator makes a specific instruction to the contrary.

Seating

Prior to an examination all students are typically lined up according to dojo protocol. Some dojos will have *Yudansha* sit opposite the exam administrator(s) separate from the *Kyudansha* who are seated facing the front.

The three most commonly used methods to bring the candidate and the primary partner together are:

1. In the first method the line of students stay seated without moving. In this case, the candidate for examination would be called out by the administrator.

2. The second method indicates the line of students has moved out of the training area, leaving the candidate and exam partner in the center of the training area. If the two are not already seated beside one another, the lowest ranking student (regardless of who is testing) would issue a formal seated bow toward the *shomen,* and sit an appropriate distance next to the higher-ranking student.

3. The third method has the administrator call out the person being graded by themselves. The candidate responds by uttering a loud and clear acknowledgment (*hai!*), then moves out to the center of the training area and sits in *seiza*. The administrator then calls out the name(s) of the partner(s) they wish to have participate. These individuals also respond with a clear acknowledgement of *hai!* and join the candidate at the center.

Examination Bowing Etiquette

A general bowing hierarchy that indicates respect (*reishiki*) is followed during an examination. At the beginning of the exam, the bows acknowledge from highest toward the lowest positions. At the conclusion the order is reversed, beginning with the lowest and moving to the highest position.

All movement during the beginning and ending bowing etiquette portion of the exam is done in *shikko* (knee walking). The candidate being examined takes the lead in all bowing etiquette.

Referring to previously described methods of being called out for the exam, if either of the first two methods are used the candidate makes a formal seated bow first towards the *shomen*, then moves in front of their partner (they will momentarily have their backs towards the Shomen, which in this instance is acceptable).

The candidate issues another formal bow to their partner, indicating an invitation out on to the training area. The partner returns the bow. The candidate then immediately moves to whichever side the administrators are seated on, leaving a space on the far side for their partner. Both move in unison toward the middle of the training area.

If the third method is employed, the candidate is already in position and the partner simply joins in.

Beginning of the Examination

Once both individuals are in the center of the training area, they issue a formal seated bow towards the *Shomen*. Then both turn slightly to face the administrator(s) and perform another formal seated bow. If the *Yudansha* have been separated from the *Kyudansha*, they issue another formal bow towards these ranking members. Finally, they turn towards one another and issue another bow.

Going forward, the administrator conducts the examination. If there's a change of partners during the exam, the candidate issues a formal seated bow to both the previous and new partner(s) as they leave or come onto the training area.

If the examination includes more than one partner, such as with *randori* (the multiple person attack/technique), etiquette requires for everyone to line up next to one another and issue a formal bow(s) in unison.

Conclusion of the Examination

Once the administrator calls for the examination's end, the candidate and their current partner return to a *seiza* position at center mat. They complete the bowing etiquette in reverse order by first issuing a formal seated bow towards each other, the *Yudansha* group if present, the test administrator(s), and finally the *shomen*.

At this point both individuals back away from the center placement using the *shikko* movement. The first step is taken continuing to face the *shomen*; thereafter, they may make a turn and quickly return to their places.

Receiving a Promotion Certificate

Depending on the examination level and organization, there's usually a period of time before rank certificates are awarded. However, the day will come when Sensei has a certificate to present, so there's a general etiquette to follow when receiving it. Knowing the proper etiquette of how to approach Sensei, bow correctly, receive the certificate, and the best way to exit is very important.

Following is a step-by-step protocol that will meet the expectations of most instructors awarding rank:

- When your name is called, respond with a loud and clear "*hai!*"

- If not already in a convenient position to *shikko* (knee walk) out to the center of the mat, stand and walk directly in front of the student line-up and stand directly in line with Sensei. Then sit down in *seiza*.

- Complete a seated bow (with eyes cast downward) to Sensei.

- *Shikko* towards Sensei, then stop within a respectful stride-and-a-half away (and wait).

- Make a slight bow towards Sensei (signaling you're in place and ready for them to begin).

- Wait and listen as Sensei reads the certificate, finishes speaking, and is ready to present the certificate.

- *Shikko* closer to accept the certificate from Sensei, and take the document in both hands.

- Move back a half step, and place the certificate on your left side.

- Complete a deep and respectful formal bow to Sensei.

- Pick up the certificate and *shikko* back to the beginning position.

- Return to your appropriate place in the line-up. If necessary stand and walk, but not before backing away from Sensei.

CHAPTER NINE

Bushido and the Aiki Spirit

Understanding Budo

Budo is a Japanese term describing all martial arts. A literal translation is the "Martial Way," and may also be thought of as the "Way of War." When O'Sensei created Aikido, he departed from the historic approach to the martial arts. And Morihei Ueshiba -- a renowned "master" -- was much sought after for his instructional skills.

O'Sensei's real-life experience as a young man placed him in various situations that proved his warrior ability; however, in his day no one questioned his *budo* as relevant or real.

What made his "new" art different from previous ones was techniques could be chosen that would not cause bodily harm or fatal injury -- a true *bushido* that resulted in a peaceful resolution.

Aiki translates to "harmonious life energy." Through his spiritual and life experience O'Sensei created an art that was not a "Way of War" but a "Way of Peace." This emphasis (particularly in his later years) resulted in countless debates over the non-violent nature of Aikido, which has resulted in the art being classified by some as "soft."

There are even individuals who question whether Aikido is even *budo*, but they have not felt the power of Aikido. Non-violence is a choice the Aikidoka makes when confronted. It is their choice to execute a technique that leaves no lasting damage to the attacker.

With this understanding, Aikidoka train with martial intent as movement is designed to incapacitate opponents. Techniques include strikes, kicks and punches known as *atemi*. There are choke holds, pressure point applications, and other techniques that can be fatal.

In weapons training, Aikidoka practice as though their wooden tools were "live blades." For instance, a wooden *jo* staff used with deadly intent is a real weapon.

It is the practitioner's choice of striking at a target that stuns and incapacitates, and can cause permanent neurological damage or fatal injury. It is "aiki" to choose the lesser of these end results.

These martial applications are often deemphasized in Aikido training class until a student is considered capable of controlling their overall movement. However, a true approach to learning Aikido always keeps a martial point of view intact.

Bujutsu is the "Science of War" or "War Craft." These definitions can be used interchangeably in the English language with the term "martial arts" (the subtlety of the terms is often lost except to scholars).

There are historical references dating before the 18th century that describe *aiki* as a stalemate situation, or one of neutrality with no win or loss. Therefore, today's Aikidoka promotes a "sense of harmony in existence."

As mentioned elsewhere in this book, different styles of Aikido earn their distinction from techniques or personal-spiritual development. Nevertheless, all *Aikido* is born from the *bujutsu* heritage, and has a solid foundation in the martial arts.

When one is serious about studying *Aikido*, they are said to follow the way of *aiki* (which refers more to the lifestyle they live and the path they walk by practicing the art).

To a casual observer this may sound almost cult-like; however, Aikido is a form of spirituality in that it allows everyone to develop a purpose while pursuing their own Aikido.

The distinction being the practicality of warfare is de-emphasized in favor of personal development from a fitness and spiritual perspective.

Ki Energy

Although all things in the Universe are made up of static or moving energy, there is constant movement even within a stationary position. Science provides a physical understanding down to the molecular level, that things are comprised of energized positive and negative elements. In the martial arts, the Tao *taijitu* opposites of **yin** (negative, dark and feminine) and **yang** (positive, bright, masculine) symbolize universal balance. In Japanese this is known as *In* and *Yo*.

Aikido generalizes this concept as *Ki*, and is synonymous with energy. Individual *Ki* – an integral form of Aikido -- is used with movement and technique, and is first learned from experiencing technical fundamentals, *kata* and various exercise.

Its importance is either emphasized or de-emphasized within the various sub-styles of Aikido, and in virtually all Aikido styles *Ki* manifests as a powerful principle. Aikido thus becomes a way to unify one's own *Ki* and mental and physical skill (frequently referred to as a "mind and body as one").

Total calm allows a practitioner to react to every situation with an appropriate response, which can be a very difficult feat to accomplish. Therefore, Aikido training includes various exercises to calm one's mind, and in this regard it is not unique among the martial arts.

Some styles advocate physical relaxation to help a person respond better to techniques. Others expound the virtues of meditative contemplation to relax the mind. Regardless of the approach, composure is fundamental to a student of Aikido in order to have a proper reaction.

The true challenge for all students is to take the principles learned from on-the-mat training and apply them to everyday life. A situation found at home with family or at work with co-workers or clients is really no different from the experience on the practice mat.

Life is a sea of storms. Some are small squalls and others are tempests. How you deal with an irate co-worker or boss is a storm. Coming home to be told by the spouse that they are leaving and filing for divorce is a storm. Being called into the boss's office to learn your job is being eliminated is a storm.

Getting a collection call from the bank because you've fallen behind on payments is a storm. Driving in rush hour traffic is a storm. Being confronted by an armed assailant is a storm. (The pressure to complete this book by a deadline was a storm!)

You're constantly faced with storms that pose as conflict; how you chose to weather those storms is where the spirit of Aiki comes into play. The Aiki spirit and following the Aiki way allows one to be centered, calm and able to make intelligent choices.

Aikido has been called the "thinking man's" martial art. Choosing humane, fair and peaceful solutions to conflict is Aikido. Therefore, you need to be resilient, make meaningful decisions and place high value on your life.

CHAPTER TEN

Fundamental Training Guide

Training with Others

Most training classes (*keiko*) are scheduled for 60 to 90 minutes in duration. At first this may appear like an ample allotment of time.

But since the class is divided into formal instruction and exercises, a student is fortunate if they have half the time to practice techniques. Therefore, knowing how to efficiently utilize class time becomes important when finding a balance in a training schedule.

Aikido requires learning from physical experience. Though you can exercise with individual *kata* movements, the majority of training involves working with at least one partner. The protocol always begins and ends the same, regardless of how many people are included in partnered training.

Begin by selecting the person with whom you wish to train, complete a seated bow, and ask them to train with you. You ask by saying *onegai shimasu* ("would you do me the favor of training?"), and their response would be to return the same gesture. You then take your place in the training area to begin the exercise that Sensei has just demonstrated.

Today's common practice will have the more senior student take the role of *nage* (who does the technique), and the junior student the role of *uke* (the attacker).

This is based on the theory that the senior student can execute the movement better to serve as an example for the junior student. However, it should be noted this is contrary to the traditional Japanese martial model where the more experienced student guides the junior student by assuming the role of attacker and taking *ukemi*.

Each individual takes four opportunities (alternating attacks left and right) to perform the technique or exercise before the partners switch roles. On signal from the instructor to cease practice, it's customary to execute a bow to your partner and thank them with "*domo arigato*," then quickly returning to a line-up spot to receive further instruction.

There are times when either the demonstrated exercise or the number of students attending class requires working with more than one person, so there are two generally accepted approaches for this type of situation:

First, three people training together begin by bowing to each other and requesting to train as previously described. The two most senior students pair up first, with the most senior person doing the technique and the other taking the role of attacker.

The third student waits in *seiza* while observing their partners train. *Nage* -- the person doing the technique -- takes four opportunities to execute the movement. Once completed, that person bows out to allow the third partner to train.

Then the third partner is included and takes the attacker role for the second training partner.

Again, *nage* has four opportunities to perform the movement, and then bows out to allow the first partner to train with the third person. In this instance, the first person takes the role of attacker for the third student who also has four opportunities to perform the technique.

This type of rotation provides everyone an equal opportunity, and allows the more senior student to guide the junior student.

An alternative for three or more people training together can use the "round" approach. The training partners begin by bowing at each other and agree to train together.

In this situation, the order of practice follows seniority. The senior-most student positions themselves in the front or middle of the group appropriate for the technique being practiced, then everyone in the group individually attacks whoever is designated as *nage*. Once everyone has completed one attack, the next person in seniority takes the role of *nage*. The round continues to allow everyone an opportunity to work with all group members quickly and efficiently.

Individual Training

Though most Aikido techniques can be practiced without a partner, individual *kata* training is a core, singular learning method. Most instructors use solo movement with at least some weapons during training; however, all technique movement can and should be practiced solo.

Practice can be applied to both sides of any technique (attack, technique and subsequent *ukemi*) as it provides a solid foundational training for the basic technique or *waza*.

CHAPTER ELEVEN

Tips for Learning

One of the first things a student of Aikido learns is there's too much information to process and not enough time to incorporate it all into a training routine.

It's important to understand that you are embarking on an educational journey, so it will take time, patience and diligence to make the "trip" worth your while.

Much of your training will involve unlearning things you've been routinely doing for years, and replacing routines with different skill sets. So in some ways it's like being a newborn as you'll learn to do everything from the beginning.

It's typical after several years of dedicated basic training to have Sensei inform you that you've developed enough fundamental skills to start Aikido training, all the while you've been working out and moving up the kyu rankings every few months. When they say "You can start training!" is when you'd receive your first *dan* (shodan) promotion and begin your real training towards mastery.

Whether you're contemplating stepping on the training mat for the first time, or have dedicated years to *budo* training, here are some tips to make the learning process more productive:

Tip 1: The Middle

Event spectators know the best viewing seat in the house is in the middle, which is why "front row, center", "fifty-yard line", "behind home plate," or "center court" is highly coveted. Most Aikido instructors usually position themselves in the center of the mat so everyone can clearly see and hear the demonstration. Taking a position in the middle also signals to Sensei that you are ready and eager to take Tip 2, *ukemi* for them.

Tip 2: Take Ukemi

While having the best seat to watch a demonstration is good, it's even better to be a part of the instruction. Aikido can best be learned through action. There's no substitute for practice, so you should train as often as possible.

Taking *ukemi* (much like the panda in the photo) from whomever is instructing the class -- as it's the best place to receive the information -- can provide invaluable information from the touch, feel and experience of the technique.

Tip 3: Train with the Demonstration's Uke

One can't always serve as *uke*, so the next best thing is to have the person who was just *uke* as your training partner, since the information they received from the instructor is fresh in their mind and body movement.

Tip 4: Mental Snapshot Method

Training your mind to observe a set pattern helps while learning movement. When observing a demonstration you can take mental "snapshots" using the following order:

- Take note of the overall attack and the instructor's response.
- Focus on the instructor's body movement and footwork.
- Observe the attacker's response to the technique.
- Note the instructor's hand and/or body movement once again.

Most instructors provide a minimum of two to four demonstrations from a variety of angle positions. If more demonstrations are offered, you should restart the "snapshot" process by focusing on more detail with each consecutive demonstration.

Then replay these pictures in your mind while you practice with your training partner.

This process works no matter what you're learning or trying to understand, because it forces you to think in "parts" while observing the "whole." This follows the adage of "How does one eat an elephant? One bite at a time."

Tip 5: Nine Times Slow -- One Time Fast

Over time Aikido movement will become a natural, instinctive motion. You'll learn to move in exactly the same manner with all the intricacy and subtleness regardless of the speed at which the movement is executed.

Learning a new technique or perfecting it is best done using a slow, continuous movement so you can focus on the nuances and subtleties of technique as well as the general movement. Movements will become embedded in your physical response over time, and you'll be able to train at increasing speeds.

When a toddler first learns to walk, they slowly rise and take very careful steps. Once sure of their movement, they become adept at running at supersonic speeds throughout the house. But they can be susceptible to occasional stumbles and falls while they're finding their footing.

You'll be incorporating this same approach in your Aikido training. To help you gain your footing you can use the nine times slow and one time fast regime (and still be able to correctly perform all aspects) while practicing your technique at a smooth, deliberate pace to reinforce the movement.

Then after having perfected the movement at a comfortable speed, you'll push yourself by performing every aspect of the technique at an increased pace just as it was done at the more relaxed speed.

By using this approach, you'll find the initial slower movement is not as slow as it once was, and movement eventually becomes natural and instinctive.

Conclusion

Nearly 80 years after Morihei Ueshiba created *Aiki Budo* as a distinct martial art, Aikido has an international fellowship of people who strive to make the world a better place by following the way of Aiki. A true *budo* (martial art), Aikido distinguishes itself by shunning the sport and competitive violence spawned by the pseudo arts popularized in televised cage fighting and computer videogames.

Yet at the same time, Aikido has risen to be recognized as a headline program at the World Combat Games. And has been popularized on television and in movies by actors like Steven Seagal -- a true Aikido master.

Aikido has an important role in continuing the legacy of the dojo culture. The world is in greater need today than ever to embrace the philosophy and approach of O'Sensei, the "Art of Peace." The Aikido culture helps shape youth, transitions adolescents to become contributing members of society, and helps adults continue self-improvement of their spiritual and physical well-being.

Aikido's path is not a solitary journey, but one that requires the help of many as you learn, train and experience the feeling of the *Aiki way*. It offers a path that all can follow, be they still in formative childhood years or someone with many years of life experience.

This book has covered key areas you'll need to firmly grasp in order to make the journey complete. Learning techniques and martial philosophy are important for Aikidoka to develop, but truly successful students also are knowledgeable of the other elements that make up the Aiki way.

Most of these elements are found in plain sight, and aren't usually mentioned unless necessary as "open secrets." They include proper etiquette, undertaking responsibilities as students, knowing the true purpose of the dojo and its role in the community, possessing and caring for training tools, understanding the Aiki spirit and fundamental training concepts. And most importantly, accepting the obligation to share well with others.

I grew up in metropolitan Los Angeles County, California, which is approximately 4,000 square miles with over 10 million inhabitants. In the early 1970s there were only three officially recognized schools teaching Aikido in L.A. that were organized by a handful of Japanese instructors who'd been besieged to spread the Aiki way throughout the United States.

During that time there were very few places for a student to have access to Aikido. An American, or anyone for that matter, wanting to learn the art had to reside in a world-class city like Chicago, London, New York, Paris, San Francisco and Washington D.C. Or they needed to live in Japan for an extended period.

In the ensuing years, numerous Aikido clubs emerged at colleges, community centers and martial arts dedicated schools. And today there are over 1,000 dojos in the U.S. that are operated by locally trained instructors. This current generation of Aikidoka has taken on the responsibility of passing the mantle of their understanding and continuing the lineage that began with O'Sensei. They're to be congratulated and commended for their efforts, because to take on this responsibility requires great personal sacrifice, dedication, and above all a quest to complete their personal Aiki journey.

If this book piqued your interest about Aikido, the best starting point is with the Sensei who are charged with passing on their knowledge and guiding you on your journey. You can ask them questions, but you need to do so in an appropriate "dojo culture" way.

As I say this, I'm reminded of the frequent admonishments from my native Japanese instructors: "You Americans talk too much. Just do (it) and you will understand (eventually)." Or, as my American trained Sensei would say, "Just shut up and train!"

Questions or Comments?

I'd love to hear your thoughts on the information provided in *An Open Secret: A Student's Handbook for Learning Aikido Techniques of Self-Defense and the Aiki Way*. Please don't hesitate to email me at **senseiwhatabout@gmail.com**.

Want to Get Aikido-Related Items?

My website **www.aikidotoday.com** is a great source for additional information on learning Aikido, reviews of other informative books and DVDs, upcoming training seminars, and links to other Aikido resources.

Japan's most famous swordsman, Miyamoto Musashi, is referred to several times throughout the book. His ***Book of Five Rings*** **(Spheres)** is considered by many authorities to be among the preeminent texts of victory over conflict.

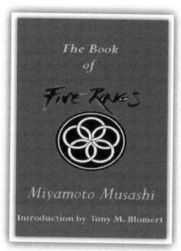

Musashi's strategies and concepts are studied in various business and martial art schools worldwide. Every martial artist and Aikidoka should become familiar with this invaluable manual that teaches budo tactics of the sword, as well as understanding the martial foundations of Aikido.

For a free download go to: http://aikidotoday.com/free-ebook/

One Last Thing...

You can learn more about me on my author profile at:
www.amazon.com/author/tonyblomert

If you believe your friends would gain something valuable from this book, I'd be honored if you'd post a review on Twitter and Facebook.

Facebook: www.facebook.com/anopensecret
Twitter: #aikido2day

Also, if you'd like to comment on how helpful and informative you found *An Open Secret*, and/or how it's contributed to your Aikido development, I'd be eternally grateful if you'd post a review on my book page from wherever you purchased or downloaded it.

Doumo arigatou gozaimashita!

References

Selected Bibliography:

Alleman, Bruce (2004): *Aikido: The essential guide to mastering the art.* Blue Snake/Frog, Ltd.

Cleary, Thomas (1999): *Code of the Samurai: A modern translation of the Bushido Shoshinshu of Taira Shigesuke.* Tuttle Publishing.

Dang, Phong Thong and Seiser, Lynn (2003): *Aikido Basics.* Tuttle Publishing.

Doi, Takeo (1973): *The Anatomy of Dependence: Exploring an area of the Japanese psyche: feelings of indulgence.* Kodansha International.

Gleason, William (1995): *The Spiritual Foundations of Aikido.* Destiny Books.

Lowry, Dave (2006): *In the Dojo: The rituals and etiquette of the Japanese martial arts.* Weatherhill/Shambahala Publications.

Musashi, Miyamoto (1993 – translated by Thomas Cleary): *The Books of Five Rings.* Shambhala Publications.

O'Connor, Greg (1991): *The Aikido Student Handbook.* Blue Snake/Frog Ltd.

Olson, Gregory D. (1996): *Aikido: A beginner's text.* Kendall/Hunt Publishing Co.

Saotome, Mitsugi (1986 – translated by Patricia Saotome): *Aikido and the Harmony of Nature.* Shambhala Publications.

Stevens, John (1987): *Abundant Peace The biography of Morihei Ueshiba*. Shambhala Publishing.

Taylor, Michael W (2004): *Aikido Terminology: An essential reference guide in both English and Japanese*. Self-published.

Tohei, Koichi (1976): *Book of Ki: Coordinating Mind and Body in Daily Life*. Japan Publications.

Turnbull, Steven (2004): *Samurai: The story of Japan's great warriors*. Metro Books, Sterling Publishing.

Ueshiba, Kisshomaru (1984 – translated by Taitetsu Unno): *The Spirit of Aikido*. Kudansha International.

Ueshiba, Morihei (2002 – translated by John Stevens): *The Art of Peace*. Shambhala Publications.

Ueshiba, Moriteru (2005 – translated by John Stevens): *Progressive Aikido: The essential elements*. Kudansha International.

Articles:

Aibudo (2014): *The Martial Arts Systems of Aibudo – Sempai/Kohai*.
http://www.aibudo.com/sem_koh/sem_koh.html

Aikido of Northern Colorado (2013):
http://www/Aikidonortherncolorado.org/

Aikikai Foundation (2000): *Aikido World Headquarters – International Regulations*.
http://aikikai.or.jp/eng/regulations/international.htm

Alvarez, Dirk (2005): *In Reverence of the Hakama.* http://www.gungfu.com/htm-resources/articles -in-reverance-of-the-hakama.htm

Bergman, Linnea (2014): *Sempai Kohai Relationships.* http://www.kendo-guide.com/sempai-kohai-relationships.html

Dease, Dan (2011): *How to Receive Your Testing Certificate.* http://www.aikiorlando.com/article/how-receive-your-testing-certificate

Goedkoop, James (1999): *Bokken, Jo, and Related Wooden Weapons.* Aikido Today Magazine May/June 1999 edition (Issue #63).

Kingfisher WoodWorks, LLC (2013): *Bokken, Jo and Other Traditional Japanese Wooden Weapons.* http://kingfisherwoodworks.com

Okumura, Shigenobu (1995): Aikido Today Magazine (Issue #41).

Tazaki, Yusei (2012): *Historical Study of Sitting in Japan: With "Seiza" as Main Topic* 2nd International Conference, Mukogawa Women's University, Nisinomiy, Japan, July 14 – 16, 2012 Proceedings.

Walsh, Robert: *How to Fold Your Gi* http://monkeyfighter.com

Wikipedia 2014 Aikido and Aikido Styles
Wikipedia 2014 Budo
Wikipedia 2014 Dan (rank)
Wikipedia 2013 Japanese Honorifics
Wikipedia 2014 Keikogi

Wikipedia 2013 Kenkyusha's New Japanese-English Dictionary, n.d. *Kancho or Soke*

Wikipedia 2014 Kyu

Wikipedia 2014 List of Standard Japanese Academic Grades

Glossary of Terms

Ai - Joining or unifying.

Aiki - Harmony or unity of body and mind.

Aikido - The way through life energy to achieve harmony and unity.

Aikidogi - Aikido uniform.

Aikidoka - Someone who lives the aiki way.

Aikiken - A wooden sword of medium weight and diameter that is well-balanced with a curvature and proportion of a real sword (katana).

Aite - Opponents/partner in training.

Atemi - A strike, hit, blow or punch.

Bokken - Wooden training sword.

Budo - The lifestyle one lives and the path they walk by practicing the particular martial art, bujutsu.

Bujutsu - A Japanese martial art developed by Samurai warriors over 800 years ago.

Bushi - Warriors.

Chugi - Loyalty, fidelity or devotion.

Daisho - Long and short sword pair used by samurai.

Daito-ryu Jujutsu - A classical school of Japanese jujutsu that traces its lineage back 1,000 years to Japan's feudal warriors, the samurai.

Dan - Dan ranks imply an acknowledged level of technical proficiency and that one is a serious student.

Deshi - Students.

Do - The way or method.

Dogi - Modern-day martial arts uniform.

Dogu - Tools or implements of the trade.

Dojo - Training hall.

Dojo cho - The "head of" or "top of" the dojo, usually the owner.

Doju kake - Weapon racks.

Domo arigato gozaimashita - Formal thank you.

Embujo or taijo - Floor space where training takes place.

Gi - Justice, righteousness or integrity.

Hajime - Begin or start.

Hakama - A pleated garment worn in Japan as either formal wear for ceremonial use as well as used in the martial arts.

Hamni handachi - Half-standing stance; technique executed with defender seated and attacker standing.

Hanbo - Short wooden weapon made to resemble a knife or short sword.

Hata - Dojo banner.

Hera - A small spatula-shaped tab sewn to the top of the back pleat in a hakama.

Himo - Straps, strings or cords.

Ikebana - Floral arrangement.

In - Japanese version for Yin energy.

Jiyu waza - Free form technique.

Jin - Humanity, charity or benevolence.

Jo staff - Cylindrical straight stick from about 50" to 56" and a diameter of about 1". It's used alone in kata, or paired with other *jo*.

Joba hakama - Training apparel that roughly translates into a horse-riding type of contraption you step into (the divided skirt makes straddling a horse easier).

Joseki - Upper side of dojo, where more senior students are seated and train.

Joza - Upper seat along the front wall.

Judogi - Judo uniform.

Kaeshi waza - Technique reversed (i.e., *uke* becomes *nage* and vice versa).

Kakemono - Calligraphic scroll on wall in shomen.

Kami - Divinity or gods.

Kamiza - Place of honor on the shomen (top seat in room).

Kancho - Founder or head of a school of martial art.

Kanji - Between 5,000 and 10,000 characters, or kanji, are used in written symbolic Japanese language.

Kata - Choreographed prearranged patterns of movements practiced either solo or in pairs.

Katana - The long-bladed sword used by all samurai.

Keiko - Formal training.

Keikogi (aka: gi) - Training uniform (aka: dogi).

Kendogi - Kendo uniform.

Kenjutsu - The art of swordsmanship. Originated with the samurai class of feudal Japan, means "the method, or technique, of the sword."

Ki (aka: qi or chi) - Basic circulating energy of life, and how to awaken it.

Kihon waza - Basic, fundamental techniques.

Kiza - Sitting stance, up on toes.

Kohai - The junior person (as opposed to senpai, the senior person).

Koshiita - Back of hakama.

Kun - Formal honorific for person of lesser stature as oneself.

Kyu rank - A grade ranking before attaining dan (black belt).

Makoto - Sincerity, honesty and reality.

Martial arts - Aiki Jitsu, Brazilian Jiu Jitsu, Hapkido, Kung Fu, Karate, Wing Chun, etc.

Meiyo - Honor, credit, glory, dignity or prestige.

Metsuke - The gaze of one's eyes.

Mokuso - A time for meditation.

Mukyu - No grade ranking, or "without grade."

Musubi - A form of harmony and peacefulness.

Nafuda kake - A rack of wooden tags identifying the names and ranks of the dojo members.

Nage - Or tori (grabber) or shite (doer); the attacker or thrower.

Obi - Belt of practice uniform.

Onegai shimasu - Formal request to either "Please receive my instruction in this way" when said by an instructor. Or "Please show me the way" when said by students.

Randori - Multiple attacker techniques. Free-style practice. The term means "chaos taking" or "grasping freedom."

Rei - Etiquette, courtesy or civility.

Reisheki - Respectfulness.

Sama - Formal honorific for anyone of equal or higher stature than one's self.

Samurai - An aristocratic Japanese warrior of a class that dominated the military aristocracy between the 11th and the 19th centuries.

San - Honorific respect for people of your rank.

Seiki - One's seat or place in the dojo.

Sensei - Teacher or instructor.

Seiza - Formal correct sitting; sitting on knees.

Senpai - Senior person (as opposed to kohai, the junior person).

Shiden - Elevated place in shomen indicating a seat of honor.

Shihan - Honorific title for expert or master instructor.

Shikko - Knee walking (aka - Samurai walk).

Shimoseki - Lower side of dojo where junior students are seated and train.

Shimoza - Lower seat or back wall opposite of the shomen.

Shinai take - Training weapon made of split bamboo.

Shisei - A posture that exudes dignity.

Shitabaki - Bottom of practice uniform, or the pants.

Shomen - The front of the dojo.

Soke - Founder or head of a martial art school.

Suburito - Training weapon made of heavy wood designed to increase strength and speed.

Sumimasen - "I am sorry" or "Please excuse me."

Suwariwaza - Seated techniques (aka: *suwate*).

Tanto - Training weapon imitating a knife.

Tatami - Mat flooring.

Tokonama - Display space located low to the ground.

Tori or shite or nage - Applies the technique during an attack during a training when throwing is applied – controls the attacking energy.

Tsuba - Hand guard on wooden *bokken* sword.

Uchi-deshi - A live-in student/apprentice who trains under and assists a sensei on a full-time basis.

Uke - Person who initiates attack; and then they must remain calm and flexible in the disadvantageous positions in which the nage places them.

Ukemi - The action of the uke after a technique is applied to them.

Uwagi (upper clothes) - The top part of the practice uniform.

Wakizashi - Short-bladed sword used by later feudal period samurai, usually a companion to the long-bladed katana.

Waza - Aikido techniques.

Yamete or matte - Stop what you're doing; wait, or hold on.

Yang - Chinese description of positive universal energy, bright and masculine in form. The opposite of yin energy, and is needed to harmonize balance.

Yin - Chinese description of negative universal energy, dark and feminine in form. The opposite of yang energy, and is needed to harmonize balance.

Yo - Japanese version of yang energy.

Yudansha - Dan graded (i.e., black belt).

Yuki - Courage, valor or bravery.

Zarei - Seated bow.

Counting to Ten in Japanese:

One – *ichi*

Two – *ni*

Three – *san*

Four – *shi*

Five – *go*

Six – *roku*

Seven – *shichi*

Eight – *hachi*

Nine – *kyu*

Ten – *ju*

About the Author

T ony Blomert is a true American Aikidoka. He was first introduced to Aikido as a college freshman over four decades ago, and still lives "the way of *aiki*" by practicing the principles in his everyday life.

He began his martial studies in Shin Shin Toitsu Aikido (1974), and received his *dan* ranking in 1978. In 1976, while still a kyu-ranked student, he was asked to instruct the Aikido section of "An Introduction to the Martial Arts" -- an accredited curriculum at Los Angeles Valley College -- by his mentor, Dr. Lynn Lomen, and Sensei Steve Munchnikov. This instructional exposure inspired his avocation of helping others learn **the Aiki way**.

A serious student of *budo*, his experience instructing others inspired his writing "The Aikidoka's World" blog from 2010 to 2013, and this book – ***An Open Secret*** -- a student's handbook to Aikido training. He also regularly contributes to the international forum www.AikiWeb.com.

Tony grew up in the Hollywood hills of Los Angeles, and became immersed in the fine arts and entertainment industries. He credits a great deal of his diversified interests on the many wonderful and talented individuals that were part of his youth.

He followed his father's footsteps with a brief career in the music industry after graduating from Hollywood High School, but was determined to take a different path.

After earning a B.A. in Political Science from the University of California Los Angeles, he went into a career in public affairs – working first in the California State Assembly, and later as a private sector consultant representing corporate clients on local and statewide matters.

In 1990, he made another career change and moved to Southern Nevada where he operated a successful swimming pool construction, renovation and maintenance company.

During his time in Las Vegas, NV Tony returned to active training with the Aikido Schools of Ueshiba (ASU) under Sensei James Sterling and attained another *shodan* ranking in 2012.

Tony lives in Montana with his wife, Eva, and their beloved Brittany upland bird dogs.

For more information about Tony Blomert and his Aikido program and products:
www.aikidotoday.com

Made in the USA
San Bernardino, CA
26 August 2017